Who's in Charge of my Mind?

Richard A. Amoedo
Philosophy Print

First Philosophy Print trade paperback edition: 2019
Revised and expanded: 2020

CONTENTS

A Message to
the Reader

A message to you, the reader. I'd like you to know that the purpose of this book is not for me to tell my story or to become well known. The purpose of this book is for you to possibly apply similarities of my life to yours. That application will allow you to see and find what I have found now for many years - which is a way to become happy and serene.

I did not know that the reason I used to be unhappy for many years was because I didn't know how to use my mind. I didn't know that my mind was being utilized against me. In retrospect, I continue to discover how my mind had been dominating me, instead of me using it.

The reason my mind used me was because no one ever taught me to use my mind. I didn't know that my mind was supposed to be like my hands and feet - there for me to manage. As a result of no one ever teaching me that, my mind became autonomous – developing automatically from society and inhibitions.

And that's how come the first 37 years of my life were miserable even when they were good. So please connect to the story, don't just read the black letters. Make it something useful for you because I don't want anybody to suffer the way that I did for 37 years out of my own ignorance. You'll see that life can and will become something that it is absolutely marvelous to enjoy, as others who have followed also discovered.

Today, even when I'm not happy, I'm peaceful and serene. And that's not to say that I'm unhappy, my state just goes from 'peaceful and serene' to 'peaceful, serene and happy!'

I wish the best for you because we all deserve that. Please see how you can assimilate your life with mine and develop your own peace of mind. Have a great adventure.

Introduction

I thought there was something wrong with me. I didn't know what it was, or why, but I could feel it. My thoughts were running 200 miles-per-hour at all times, and the thoughts that came to me were almost entirely negative.

I initially believed the problem was the negative thoughts. But I didn't understand the underlying problem: these negative thoughts came without any desire or effort on my part. It was as if these thoughts were built into me, a part of me, and totally out of my control.

No matter how much or how little I had, no matter how much I had achieved, I suffered. No matter how much I fought against these thoughts, I lost. They simply manifested, constantly and effortlessly, and I had no peace. Do you see yourself in that?

Eventually, as explained in the pages which follow, I began to see that my mind was operating without me. I wasn't in control of my own mind, and if I wasn't in control of it, then who was?

That is the reason for the name of this book.

Who's in charge of my mind?

This was the question which needed to be answered, and the problem which needed to be understood.

The more I grew in my understanding, the more I began to correct my misthinking. I call it misthinking because thinking is utilized for constructing and that's not what my mind was doing with people or with me. *The more I changed my misthinking into thinking, the more I began to find peace.*

That is the reason the story of my development, and how I began to manage my mind (most of the time), continues as follows.

Chapter 1

By the age of 37

By the age of 37, I had five stores, a brand-new Porsche 928, three houses, a wife, a son, and two girlfriends. Although I possessed more than ever before, I had nothing because I didn't have myself. My mind was unmanageable. Obsessive thoughts, intrusive thoughts, and the constant nagging of my fears and insecurities were driving me crazy.

I was in a constant struggle to get **more**, and **more was never enough**. I didn't even realize how insane I was.

One of the girlfriends suffered from alcoholism. I had become obsessed with her, and this obsession began to affect every aspect of my life. In an effort to save her from her addiction, she had been sent to Hazelden, which is a treatment facility in Minnesota.

One day, I had the good fortune of receiving a questionnaire in the mail. It was about the girlfriend; the professionals at Hazelden wanted to find out what I knew about her. In my "tremendous wisdom" I decided that if I went there myself, I could better tell them how to fix her.

By this time, I was out of control. My emotions had become distorted and unbalanced. One minute I was up, the next I was down. I was irrational and irritable. I had always been able to control my emotions but now found that to be impossible.

On the flight to Minnesota, as I was looking out the window at the clouds, a thought came to me. It was the first sane thought I'd had in quite some time.

The thought was, *Richard, the problem is not with her. The problem is with you.*

You need help.

It was the first time this realization had occurred to me. And although I didn't realize it at the time, admitting I had a problem and asking for help was the first step to getting well, and the first step toward developing a saner life.

When I arrived at Hazelden, my first objective was to locate her counselor, but when I found him, I was no longer thinking that I could help with the girlfriend.

What I told him instead was, "I came here to tell you how to fix her, and realized I need help. Would you help me, please?"

It was late in the day, and the office was closing. The counselor gave me directions to a nearby hotel and told me to get some rest, then call him in the morning.

People often say it'll get worse before it gets better, and that night it got worse because I tried to solve the problem myself. I went for dinner but couldn't eat. I decided instead to go back up the hill to the hotel because there was a bar on the lower level. On my way up, I saw a tractor-trailer approaching on the highway and thought seriously of jumping in front of it. I reasoned that if I did this, then she would come to see me.

I made my way to the bar and ordered a scotch. I forced myself to drink the first one but lost interest in the second. I didn't want to do anything. I didn't want to be anywhere. And by the time I made it back to my room, my mind was on a rampage. I was pacing, I was frantic, and I was miserable.

I went to the window and looked to the mountains. Then I fell to my knees, supplicating, saying, **"GOD, please help me!**

Whatever is affecting me right now shouldn't be, but it is! GOD, please help me!"

But I wasn't yet ready for help, and after my prayer, the insanity came back.

By the time the night was over I had decided I was "too well" for help. Hazelden wasn't going to accept me. They were trying to help her, not me.

That morning, as the counselor instructed, I called the office. While waiting on hold, I thought about the situation. I knew they wouldn't take me. But when the counselor picked up the line, he said, "I have a place ready for you. Come on in."

At that moment, between my cries, I began saying, "Thank you, thank you, thank you."

That was all I could do.

As I started for Hazelden, something magical happened, a miracle, unlike anything I had ever experienced. When I got in my car, for the first time in my life, I realized I wasn't alone. I was by myself, indeed, but I could feel a presence in the vehicle.

It was the first time I realized there was a GOD.

I went to the facility, checked in, and was soon introduced to a discussion group. After that one, I joined a second group. By this time, another level of reality had become clear to me. I realized I had met up with the most ignorant human being in the world, and it was me. I don't mean ignorant in the sense of not being intelligent. Rather, *I saw that I didn't know how to live life in a satisfying way* – a way where I could be satisfied with reality.

I also witnessed something I had never seen before: people were talking about their feelings. I needed to realize what my feelings were as well as the feelings of others.

I had not been a human *being*.

I had been a human *doer*.

And I realized something else. There was a reason I had become what I had become. There was a reason for my unhappiness and discontent. The reason was my secrets — two of them, to be precise. Two terrible secrets I intended to take to the grave with me.

I had never shared these secrets with anyone.

One of the things these groups practiced was the sharing of personal stories. It was amazing to see these brave individuals sharing their struggles, and traumas, and hopes. Telling their stories seemed to help them heal in some way, and so, by the third or fourth day, I decided to tell mine.

That night, while waiting for the group to start, I found myself wanting to share my story with as many people as possible. I began inviting more people to join.

I saw a few young women standing to one side, and so I went to them and said, "I'm about to tell my life story. Would you come and listen to it? I want to punish myself even more."

The girls joined the group, and I began to speak.

Two Secrets

The first secret I swore to never speak of was that I had been raped by a teenager when I was five years old.

The second was that I was raped again, by an uncle, when I was eight.

Shedding light on these two secrets was highly emotional, and as I spoke, I began to cry. But then a weight lifted. The group listened with empathy, and after a short time, I began to experience something I never had before; a weight being lifted from me.

I had always hated the cold, and this was Minnesota in February. It was miserably cold outside, and yet I was full of vitality. Everything felt wonderful, and new, and exciting. I could look at the sky and feel like I was a part of it. I was the first one to get up in the morning and the last one to go to sleep at night, and still, I had energy to burn. It was as if something inside had taken me over, and it was incredible.

But no transition is instantaneous. Because of my connection to the girlfriend, the counselor had placed me on the side for family and friends, and even there my mind played tricks on me.

One of the ongoing battles I had experienced throughout my life was the feeling of unrest and unease. My mind was constantly going, and no matter the problem, when I found a solution, I would immediately find another problem.

Another irritation.

Another frustration.

One of these problems occurred to me on my next to last day at Hazelden. It was the question of my sexual orientation.

Richard, maybe you're gay.

For the next few hours, this thought drove me crazy. I questioned myself and wrestled with the idea, but I was also aware of this new understanding of reality, and of GOD. I knew He could help me with this difficulty, and so I reached out to Him.

What came to me was, **Richard, you have always screwed yourself. Do you have any desire to be with a man?**

No.

Have you ever wanted to be with a man?

Well, no.

I considered this and began to reflect on my life. When I was young, twelve or thirteen, and I started to hear about the birds and the bees, it brought back memories of what had happened when I was five and eight. I didn't know how to process this new understanding of those traumas, and so, at twelve or thirteen, I made the decision that my mind was going to be the strongest force on earth. Nothing was ever going to bother or affect me.

And for the most part, I was successful, until the age of 37. But with the trauma of what had happened to me came another problem I didn't expect or understand; sexual insecurity.

Even though I had heard the phrase, "Size doesn't matter," for men it matters, and for me at that young age, it **really** mattered. I became concerned that my equipment wasn't sufficient. I wondered what was normal, what was average, and what was **enough**, for several years, until I was able to get a book which explained things in detail.

I looked up the average dimensions and discovered I was above that, so I said, "Wonderful!"

But these dimensions were regarding a man in an aroused state, and so a new concern came to me. What about an unaroused state?

When is small too small?

I began having sex at the age of nineteen, but it was never about making love. It was about proving I was a man. And my insecurity never left me. After sex, I would turn away, or move to the side. Even though I could function normally during the act, the thought would always return afterward.

When is small too small?

I had wrestled with these thoughts my entire life and had even gone to psychiatrists as a result. But that day, my second to last at Hazelden, I found something I never had before.

With my new understanding of GOD, I found strength, I found comfort, and I found my insecurity lifted from me. My old misunderstanding of GOD was only that there had to have been a GOD because someone must have created this crap. In Hazelden, I came to see that I had been protected in the past (even when I didn't know it or appreciate it), that GOD continues to protect me in the present, so subsequently I have arrived at the certainty that GOD will always take care of me.

This realization was the product of looking back at the times GOD had saved me and performed miracles in my life. When those miracles had occurred, I had disregarded them and either attributed my protection to luck or told myself that I would wait to *really believe* in GOD when the next miracle occurs. I'm grateful I stopped waiting.

One reason for my gratitude is that my last headache was February 17th, 1986. I used to get headaches, but I came to understand that the source of those headaches were my secrets. There is a toll to pay for maintaining secrets, and I had been paying it for a long time.

When I let go of those secrets, there were no more headaches; No headaches, no allergies, no hemorrhoids.

And what's more, this was the very beginning of my journey to peace, tranquility, and happiness. I still had a lot to learn, but it was a pretty good deal for getting well, and letting go of garbage.

Growing old is mandatory; growing up is optional. I'm glad I chose to exercise the option.

Deny Entry

I left Hazelden but continued to attend group gatherings, and for the first six weeks or so everything was good, largely because I didn't know any better. But as it happened, I began to notice that the people in my group weren't very happy.

I wanted to be happy and started thinking to myself, *I can do this on my own. I didn't need any help being unhappy.*

Many members of the group had trouble with alcohol abuse. After attending this group for a while, I realized I didn't have a problem with alcohol. My problem was self-sabotage; a result of those two secrets, as well as the false and injurious beliefs, inculcated within me since infancy.

I enjoyed the group, though, and I felt comfortable there. And the group would get a kick out of me when I would introduce myself.

"I'm Richard," I would say. "And I'm leaning toward alcoholism."

I was blessed when it came to substance abuse, in part due to the decision I made at twelve or thirteen that nothing would overcome my mind. Alcohol couldn't overcome me, and neither could drugs. When I tried pot, all I got from it was a headache. Cocaine resulted in nothing more than an itchy nose. And I thank GOD for this because I've seen the damage addiction can cause. If I had become addicted, I might still be in that situation. Or dead.

As I continued to read and study, I began to see that most of my thoughts were negative. I knew I needed to rid myself of that, but I didn't know how.

I was still in the dinette business at that time, with five stores, box trucks, vans, around forty employees, and a large inventory to catalog and track. The stores were linked via fax machines, with the merchandise tracked by computer.

There was a woman working for me at the time, a computer operator from China, who helped with this task. When it was time to input inventory in the system, I would call out the information, and she would enter it. One day, an error occurred while she was typing, and a message appeared in the upper-righthand corner of the screen.

Deny Entry.

In my "tremendous wisdom," I thought, ***Well, hell. If it works for the computer, maybe it'll work for me.***

So after that, anytime a negative thought occurred to me, I would say to myself, "Deny Entry."

But there was a problem with this method, and the problem was this; I hadn't replaced my negative thoughts with positive thoughts. Instead, I had created a vacuum, and anytime one creates a vacuum, something must fill it. So after a few days of saying this, **Deny Entry** itself had become a negative and obsessive thought.

It was driving me crazy, but I've always been a persistent man, and anytime I've persisted with something good I've succeeded. Eventually, I began to succeed with this, as well.

Will

I was born in Argentina and came to the United States at the age of 17. Thus, prior to my involvement with this group of people, I really didn't know how to read or write English. I could speak the language and was reasonably good at talking to others, but my communication skills were quite limited.

I hated feeling like a foreigner, and I *really* hated sounding like one. I had no one to teach me, so I taught myself. Being that I was my own teacher, I could only work with what I had at my disposal. So, anytime I came across a word I didn't understand, I looked it up.

I was methodical about this, and my understanding of the English language began to grow. After a while I discovered something incredible; the thing I hated most was, in fact, a tremendous asset. Not only had it forced me to build a large vocabulary, but it also taught me to find the true meaning of words most native speakers take for granted. After some time of doing this, I began to realize I knew the language better than many Americans!

One of the words I came across in the course of my studies was the word *will*.

Will this.

Will that.

What the hell is this? I thought. *There are people named Will, so what is this will?*

So I looked it up and saw that **will is an action in past tense**. Suddenly things I couldn't do before, like turn my will and my life over to the care of GOD, began to make sense. I realized I could turn my actions and my life over to the care of GOD, as I began to understand those actions. All I needed to do was look at those actions and make sure they were positive. If they weren't positive, then I needed to correct them.

As I reflected on my life and behaviors, I began to realize how self-centered and narcissistic I had been. But I didn't stop with these realizations. I started making changes.

I wanted to become a good human being, and as I scrutinized each action, and made efforts to correct my behavior, I began to develop the positive attributes I sought. And as I grew in trust, I started to grow in my relationships as well.

About a year after I first joined the recovery group, I heard something for the first time that never before had I heard or even considered. The quote has been attributed to many people but has its origins in ancient Eastern philosophy, and when I first heard it, I stopped in my tracks.

"The thinking mind is a wonderful servant or a horrible master."

I thought, **you mean to tell me my mind is supposed to be working for me?**

I was astonished by this insight, and I realized then that, despite my progress, my head was still not working for me. I had learned, and I was growing as a person, but I still was not living with an abundance of good thinking. When I made this discovery, I realized how pitiful I still was, and how much I had yet to learn.

(How is it that I'm just sitting around minding my own business and all of a sudden, I'm in a conversation with somebody that isn't there, and I don't even want to talk to them?!)

Chapter 2

Understanding

Prior to these revelations, I was never present. Wherever I was, I was never truly there. I was either in the past or the future, thinking about what I didn't get, what I wanted, how things should have been, and why they weren't that way. And I couldn't communicate well with anyone because I couldn't truly listen.

Anytime someone spoke to me I began establishing in my head what I thought they were trying to say, how I would reply, and how they didn't know what the hell they were talking about anyway. I began to understand that this was a horrible way to communicate with anyone because what I was doing was not communication.

In order to fix this, I found a communications course and signed up. The course was not only verbal but physical, as well, and it taught me to hear communications without the distortion of emotion. My ability to converse with others improved significantly, and I realized just how poor my communication skills had been.

One example of poor communication occurred early in my marriage. I was sitting in the living room watching tv when my wife at the time began talking to me. I don't know how long she spoke — it seemed like five or ten minutes — but when she finished, she started all over again. The same thing, on and on and on.

One of the things that used to control my life was my anger, and when she began to repeat herself, I exploded.

"What? Do you think I'm stupid? I heard everything you said!"

Through the communications course, I began to understand what had happened. I hadn't acknowledged her. I hadn't given her any feedback. I didn't even nod in her direction. She had no way of knowing I had heard anything she said. Poor communication skills, indeed. And poor relationship skills.

The course outlined two types of acknowledgments: half acknowledgments; and full acknowledgments. Half acknowledgments make a person talk and indicate that I am listening. These include 'uh-huh,' 'ok,' 'mm-hmm,' and others. Full acknowledgments end a person's communication when I respond with 'yes,' 'no,' 'I understand,' or something similarly definitive.

The course also taught me how to communicate with children, and how to train them. Children had always gotten the best of me, and the reason was simple; I was more of a child than they were, and I was equally reactive. But I learned how to speak to them effectively, and how to properly correct them, without anger or frustration. Proper communication required me to grow up first - remember growing old is mandatory; growing up is optional.

During the course we were asked a question: Have you ever started reading, and found that, at the bottom of the page, you couldn't recall what you had just read?

Sure, I thought. **Who hasn't?**

Then they presented a sentence utilizing an uncommon and very strange word. Until the word was defined and understood, the sentence made no sense. Additionally, at that word, I stopped comprehending and could not understand the rest of the message. The point of this exercise was to show that effective communication requires **understanding**. Through this, I learned never to pass a word that wasn't fully understood, because to do so creates a void in my mind that doesn't allow me to retain what I was reading or hearing.

The word understanding is incredibly powerful to me. Now, this may not be factual as I remember it, but the word **understand** (as I understand or misunderstand) comes from the Greek language, and in its full context means to **stand safely under the tree**. I considered this and began to ask how it applied to my life.

I came to see that when I was alright with something and didn't have a problem with it, it was because I had an understanding of the situation. It may be unpleasant, and I may not like it, but if I have an understanding of it, then I'm okay with it.

On the other hand, when I have a misunderstanding, then I don't feel safe. Fear leads to worry and soon I'm all over the place, mentally as well as emotionally.

Understanding is powerful because it gives me the ability to be at peace. And when I am not at peace, I know I have a misunderstanding, for which more research is needed on my part to develop an understanding, so that I may be safe and at peace.

Spirituality

Around this time I began hearing a lot about spirituality.

What the hell is spirituality? I thought.

So I looked it up, and the first definition I found was that spirituality ***gives life to the physical***. I began to understand what this meant because when I first came into contact with reality, I was ***lifted from within***. That first week at Hazelden I had energy to burn, as well as my new understanding of GOD, but I still had no knowledge of spirituality.

Then one day I was listening to a man speak, and he gave me a second definition. The definition he gave was that ***spirituality was the highest form of reality there is***. In light of this, I began to develop new understandings and a new sense of reality.

I like to think of levels of well-beingness in terms of working a job. I've never been afraid of change, and anytime an employer would not advance me, I would go somewhere else and advance myself. Toward the end of my career as an employee, I worked as a troubleshooter, both electrically and mechanically, on highspeed packaging equipment.

When I went someplace to apply for a job because my current employer would advance me no further, they would ask if I had ever worked on equipment like the kind they were operating. To this, I would say, "No. Nor did I know about the equipment I have been working with prior to seeing it or working with it for the first time."

Then I would say, "Let me tell you how it is with me. My first month here, I'm just going through the motions. I do the best I can with what I know, which won't be much. By the time I've been here three months, I'll be pretty good. And by the time I've been here six months, I'll be as good or better than the best worker you have."

That's the way it was throughout my career as an employee, and this is how it is with understanding and recognizing various levels of well-beingness.

When I was younger, I would try to go dancing. Seeing as how I was not a dancer, I was always shy and afraid to ask anyone to dance with me. I would usually spend the whole night talking to myself about what I was going to do and with whom, without ever doing anything besides hold up the wall.

But as I began to develop an understanding regarding this, I began to realize my fears and insecurities were misplaced, because most people are only concerned with themselves. If I could just forget myself and have fun, whether I danced well or not would be irrelevant. I had to get outside of myself, and that was the first reality. Of course, the second reality was that I wasn't really there to dance, I was there to find a woman.

As I progressed, I moved from one level of reality to another and another. I also began to learn about and develop an understanding of spiritual principles. What you sow is what you reap? What does that mean?

If I'm a thief, there's a good possibility I'm going to end up in jail, or worse. If I cheat, there's going to be a consequence. If I'm dishonest with others, or myself, there will be repercussions.

As I progressed in my studies, I was exposed to other spiritual principles, such as *as a man thinks it in his heart, so is it.*

For instance, every relationship I had that ended was ended long before the final goodbye. It was ended early on with my thinking.

This is not going to work out. This can't go on.

And usually, the relationship lasted too long because either I, or she, did nothing to correct or end it in the beginning.

One of the stories I love the most is about a guy who goes to see his psychiatrist every week, and every week he tells the psychiatrist about his wife, and how awful she is.

Finally, one day, he goes to the psychiatrist and says, "Doctor, you've got to help me with my wife. She's ungrateful, she's rude, and I'm at my wit's end. It just can't go on!"

The psychiatrist looks at him calmly and says, "Why not? It's been going on for ten years."

An understanding of these principles and development through them does not come easily or quickly. At certain times I've tried to develop something with my mind without first believing in it, but without belief, it seldom works.

Why are spiritual principles so important? I asked myself.

But to get at the answer, I had to better understand the concept.

Spiritual Principles

A spiritual principle is a truth. It cannot be changed by anyone or anything. It makes no difference if the whole world disagrees, these truths cannot be bargained or reasoned with.

The first principle is **What you sow, you reap.**

If I plant a potato, I'm going to get potatoes. Not tomatoes, not grapes, not zucchini. And as I grew in my understanding of this, I realized I needed to learn how to operate within these principles.

Another of these truths is, **as a man thinks it in his heart, so is it.**

Whenever I recognize that I'm telling myself something from the old repertoire, I change it. For instance, when I'm speeding down the highway and pass a police car, I sometimes strike up a conversation in my mind about whether I'm going to get pulled over. I learned to recognize when I am doing this, and to end the conversation the moment I become aware of it.

Instead of worrying and glancing back at the mirror, I instead say, "Thank you, GOD."

Why am I thankful? Because I haven't had too many speeding tickets in my lifetime - certainly not as many as I deserved. And I've received even fewer since I stopped conversing with myself about getting a ticket before a ticket has even occurred.

I thank GOD for taking care of me, and I continue on my way.

And what about the times I have been stopped? No big deal. Once I was stopped, and the officer asked why I was going so fast. I told him it was Sunday, I was feeling good, and I was just stepping on the gas. He replied that he had let me go about a month before, but he was going to give me one today.

On the other hand, I was pulled over once by a policewoman. She asked, "Didn't you see me behind you?"

I said, "No, I'm sorry. I had my head up my ass. I didn't notice until you turned on the sirens."

I don't know whether she laughed, but she didn't give me a ticket.

The deal is that even when I do get a ticket, I thank GOD for all the tickets I deserved but didn't get.

It's also this way with gambling. I used to go to Vegas, and when I went, I would take money "to lose". At least that's what I would tell myself. *I'm bringing $2,000 to lose.*

And that's precisely what I did. I lost it. But a funny thing happened when I stopped framing my thoughts that way. I started winning.

One thing I've come to realize through these experiences is that I can make a mountain out of a molehill, or I can make a molehill out of a mountain. It's up to me, and it all begins with what I think, and believe, and say.

I don't know how many spiritual principles exist. Perhaps there are only a few, but a few are all we need to cover most everything.

What you sow, you reap.

What doesn't that cover?

As a man thinks it in his heart, so is it.

What doesn't that cover?

Those two, to me, encompass nearly everything. There's a line in a book I study that speaks of **the discovery that spiritual principles will solve all of my problems.**

The key to this statement isn't even the part about spiritual principles, but the word **discovery**.

The definition of **discover** is **to search and study**.

There was a process which enabled me to get to this level of happiness, and that process was dependent upon research and study. It's the same as writing a book. There's a process. It's not that I wake up one morning, start writing, and then head to the press. It takes work and diligence.

It can sometimes be difficult to recognize the implications of these principles because the results are seldom a one-to-one correlation. When I plant a seed, the sprout isn't going to come up exactly as I envision it. It may be a little to the left or a little to the right. So a person may steal, but that doesn't mean they will have the same exact thing happen to them. Perhaps what is stolen from them is love, or personal wellbeing, or peace, or tranquility.

There is someone I'm partnered with that demonstrates how much a person can grow just by side-stepping the mistakes I made and following a good course. In less than 1 year, he is experiencing what it took me 10 years to develop. When I met him, he was about 12 years old emotionally. Now, in 1 year, he's about 23 or 24 emotionally. At 28 years of age, he's already experiencing a sense of empathy, duty, and love that I didn't know in my first year of development – and he's already enjoying the fruits of that evolvement.

I picked up a sign from an estate sale a few weeks ago. It says, ***the man who kneels before GOD can stand up to anything.***

That's a way of life for me.

All of the time?

No.

Enough of the time for me to live a free life?

Yes.

And the reason I'm so free is because I've come to understand the power of spiritual principles and because *I've put in the necessary work and dedication to develop understanding and remove all of the junk from my life.*

Clearing out Junk

It took a number of years before I realized how blessed we all are, and how blessed I am.

One of the biggest miracles I experience daily, and in every moment if I choose to, is the ability to be at peace with anything and everything. The things that used to trouble me, the secrets that bossed me around for over 37 years, all of it no longer bothers me.

For a long time, I was the biggest detriment to myself, and today nothing bothers me the vast majority of the time. If something does annoy me, it's usually for only a moment, which is nothing to even complain about. But to reach this state of peace and tranquility, I first had to clear the junk out of my life.

Part of this process involved a close examination of my past and the history of my prior development. One of the things I realized during this examination was that I had come from a very "normal" family. My mother wanted twelve children, and my father wanted none. When my oldest sister was born, my father left for a little while. When I was born, he left for a little bit longer. And when my youngest sister was born, he left altogether.

My parents were two very strong minds who never connected properly before marriage, and the ones who paid the most were the children, all three of us.

My mother was a good woman, but her emotions were erratic. One moment we might find her singing, and a moment later she could become hell on wheels. She was stubborn, which is one of the good things I picked up from her. My stubbornness has allowed me to persist in many ways and against a variety of obstacles. One of the things I never wanted to be was stupid, and while I was at Hazelden and realized I had met up with the most ignorant human being in the world (and that it was me), it was my stubbornness that gave me the persistence to remove that ignorance.

I grew up in Argentina, which was quite cosmopolitan at that time. I was an incredibly shy child, and although I was not small for my age, I was bullied. Despite the ongoing abuse from bigger kids, I had a fire inside, and I could only be bullied to a certain point. Once I was painted into a corner, I would come out fighting, and when that happened, I usually won.

The thing I noticed about my father was that he was a runner. If there were too many difficulties, he took off. My mother, on the other hand, was a fighter, even when there was nothing to fight about.

Once I was listening to a tape by Scott Peck, and he was talking about *character disorders* and *neurotics*. A person with a character disorder, he explained, assumes no responsibility. That individual thinks, just as I did, that he or she will be well when the rest of the world gets its stuff together. But the rest of the world never gets its stuff together, and so the individual never does, either.

A neurotic person, on the other hand, assumes responsibility for everything, even if the fault isn't theirs. I was not a neurotic, and my mother wasn't, either. We both had a character disorder.

When I realized that my character disorder came from my mother, I went to have a talk with her. It was the first and only real talk my mother and I ever had. There was nothing like that before, and nothing after.

I asked her to remember her childhood and to tell me how it was when she was growing up. I knew she would remember, and she did.

After listening for about ten minutes, I concluded that my character disorder didn't come from my mother at all. It came from my grandparents. So, after she spoke a while longer, I asked if she remembered her grandparents, which would have been my great-grandparents.

She said she did and continued on. After another ten minutes, I began to establish that it wasn't my grandparents, either. It was my great-grandparents who were responsible for the way I was.

But then I realized where this was headed, and the next logical step in this line of reasoning. As far back as I wanted to go, I could find fault and place blame. So I made a decision at that moment.

I told myself, **Richard, it makes no difference where you got your junk from. The chain is broken now.**

And I began to break that chain, and assume responsibility; even for things that weren't mine. I even assumed responsibility for the rapes I had experienced from the teenager and my uncle.

I had begun in left field and had now moved to right field. The goal was to find balance and make my way to center field.

Although I only spoke with my mother once about her past, it helped me understand her. One thing I realized was that what she had wasn't hers, and what I had wasn't mine; the junk, the garbage, the false beliefs. She didn't know how to get rid of hers, but I learned how to get rid of mine.

One word I came across around this time was the word **sober**, so I looked it up. One definition was **not being under the influence**, but depending on the thickness of the dictionary, there could be 5, 10, even 15 definitions for the word sober. I noticed that all of these definitions had something in common.

They were all about *balance*.

That struck me the most because balance was something I never had. For me, anything worth doing was worth doing to an extreme. I never went for half-measures.

Anger and Rage

One of the first things I needed to rid myself of was my anger. For a long time, my life was controlled by my anger and rage.

I had been on this new path of growth and development for a few months when, one day, I had a disagreement with my then-wife. Before this time, there had been very few disagreements between us because I wouldn't tolerate it. But as things progressed, and as I developed and changed, she became bolder in that respect.

I had never allowed anyone I perceived as weaker than me to disagree or put their decision above mine. As she became emboldened, we found ourselves at odds over a particular employee. The employee had been giving opinions over what to do with the business, and I wanted to fire him. She didn't want to fire him, and at that time it was still not a good thing for a woman to disagree with me.

We were in her office when this occurred, and I couldn't tolerate it. In my rage, I began to destroy her office, and only stopped short of putting the desk on top of her.

A few months later we found ourselves in the same situation. She disagreed with me, and I stood up to begin rearranging her workspace, but this time something was different. This wasn't the choice I wanted to make. It wasn't the path I wanted to follow.

"I can't do this again," I said, knowing something had to change. "Either you go, or I go. What's it going to be?"

She told me she didn't want to go, so I said I would.

I remember it was a Wednesday. I told her I would be back the following Thursday and that she could make a decision then.

I came back the following week and asked her what it was going to be, but she didn't know. Being that a clear sense of reality was something I had not fully developed, but was only beginning to understand, the statement I made next was this:

"You take the houses, you take the stores, you take the Porsche 928. I'll take $5,000."

I didn't have any other assets or accounts. $5,000 was all I would take to start fresh.

She agreed to that, although she did give me the Porsche – with the $1,050 a month payment – and $3,500 to start fresh. Our business was worth a great deal at the time, but to begin ridding myself of my anger and rage, this was the price I was willing to pay.

As time progressed, I tried various ways to change my temperament. Every time an explosion occurred, I would decide never to let it happen again. And that worked fine when only one thing happened. But then two things would happen, and I would explode again.

So then I decided that even if *two* things happened, I wouldn't explode. The result? I would blow on the third thing.

When I finally recognized this pattern, I decided that no matter what occurred, I wasn't going to explode. Three things, four things, a dozen things. It didn't matter what the problem was, or how many there were, I would maintain my composure.

Eight or ten months later I found myself in my car, wanting to get mad as hell, but I couldn't.

I came to understand that when I get mad at something, I'm not truly mad at that particular thing. What I'm upset about is my own internal preconception, and how that relates to the thing in question. My anger, therefore, has nothing to do with the reality of the situation.

I remember a story Dr. Wayne Dyer used to tell about being in Hawaii and going outside each morning to do yoga and center himself. One morning he went outside to do just that and came across a man tending the garden with a weed-eater.

When Dr. Dyer told the story, he would say, "I am trying to meditate and get centered and become a whole person, and there's this guy with a weed-eater!" The point being that if we wait for the right circumstances to become a whole person, we will never become whole.

There will always be interferences. What I needed to learn was how to remove those interferences without having an emotional response to them.

In the beginning, one of the things I noticed was this: I would be enjoying my life until a curve would come. . . and when it did, *I became furious!*

At first, I didn't know why, but then I learned why. I had gotten to this marvelous stage of wholeness I had always desired, and now some 'inconsiderate fool,' or some 'ridiculous inconvenience,' had come to disturb 'my kingdom!'

So, I made a decision; whenever a problem came my way, I would not allow myself to be disturbed by it. The result of that decision was an important realization. I had always claimed to be an independent person, yet anything at all had the power to upset me. Traffic, a rude cashier, *anything at all*.

What kind of independence is that?

I was so egotistical that when I was in the zone, I thought the whole world needed to stop for me and bend to my unspoken desires.

In reality, when I give anything the ability to upset me, it's a disservice to GOD. Not because I'm putting myself in GOD's place, but because I'm now putting **things with no value** in GOD's place, which is even worse.

Anything that overtakes my emotions becomes my GOD, and the worst part is that most of the time, it was the negative things that overcame me. I gave power to things that had no power. At least if they were positive things, it would be less of an insult. If it were my father or mother or sister or son, that would be different, because those things have value. But a cashier, or a rude waitress, or a slow driver?

This has been the process in all things. I couldn't make a blanket statement that I was going to be good in all aspects of my life because that would be too general. I couldn't be good at **one** thing, sometimes, much less **everything**.

But through a steady and continual process of identification and elimination, I have gotten consistently better. And eliminating these unwanted aspects has encouraged further development and wellbeing.

(How is it that I'm driving around and all of a sudden, I'm starting a conversation with a policeman about a ticket and I haven't even seen a cop? Why do I need to have a conversation about that?)

Chapter 3

Silver Spoons and Courage

My father left by the time I was nine-years-old. We were living at his mother's house at that time, and one of the things I resented most about my father was the position in which he placed me. He was an oral surgeon, and as the son of an oral surgeon, I was supposed to be the boy with the silver spoon. When he was at his practice, things were well. He treated and cared for the socialites and elites of Buenos Aires.

But he was also a confused man and didn't tend to his practice as he should have. Every so often a friend of his would come around with a new venture. My dad would leave his practice and sink all of the money he had saved into this new venture. That friend's name was Richard. That's where I got my name.

Things were difficult with my father gone. I began working by the age of ten or eleven, but I could only do simple jobs, such as running groceries for the local store. And nothing I earned could ever cover the expenses of our daily living.

So, I began to steal.

I stole quite a bit, and that's how we survived for a long time. One of the funny things about this, however, is I never liked doing it. It always felt wrong to me, and of the hundreds of times I stole, only twice was it for myself and for something other than necessities. Once, it was shirts for our soccer team, and the other time was a bicycle for me.

I was fearful of getting caught but continued stealing in spite of that fear. That's how I came to know about courage. So often we think of courage as being fearless, and doing something without feeling afraid, but that's not courage. ***Courage is doing something in spite of being afraid***.

That's also how I learned the difference between being fearful and being fearless. Fearless is when I do something even though I have a fear about it. Fearful is when that fear stops me.

Being fearful has stopped me from doing many wonderful things in my life. For many years my fearfulness even stopped me from writing this book.

We didn't have a tv in those days, so we went to a lot of movies. The films were shown in two blocks, one which started around one o'clock and ended at seven, and another that started at seven and ended around one. You could watch three movies during that time, and it was fairly inexpensive.

The movies I saw were generally American, and if I was not watching American movies, I was reading books about World War II, which, of course, included America. As I got a little bit older and began to know about women, I realized I liked American women.

To the best of my recollection, I began to be an American by the time I was nine years old. I just didn't arrive in America until I was seventeen.

The way I came to the U.S.A. was by first making my mother's life miserable for about two years. I was around fifteen years old at this time. I was working at a grocery store, and sometimes with my uncles. Whatever money I made – and it was often the only money we had – would only cover about two or three days of food. I wasn't too eager to continue living that way, and from the age of nine, I had wanted to come to the United States. At one point I thought I had found my escape in joining the Merchant Marines, but to enter you had to be at least 16, and I wasn't old enough. That's when I began to make my mother's life difficult until she finally decided to come to the United States as a housekeeper.

After a year-and-a-half, maybe two, she sent the money for me to fly from Argentina to New York City. I arrived with all the delusions of a teenager, thinking that when I landed at JFK International Airport, the president of the United States and Ann Margaret would be there to greet me. Neither was waiting for me upon arrival and the following day I was working as an electrician's helper for a buck and a quarter an hour.

I got over my delusions pretty quickly.

So, although my mother sent the money for me to come to America, I wouldn't say she brought me here. I like to say instead that I sent my mother here first.

When I came to the states, the thing I disliked the most was my accent. I wanted to be an American so badly. I didn't want anybody to recognize my accent. I wasn't terribly successful in that regard, but you have to consider the teacher. My teacher didn't know what the hell he was doing. He never got a diploma. He barely made it out of primary school.

That teacher was me.

I suppose I became an American as a result of John Wayne, Ann Margaret, westerns, war stories, and the like. There were always heroes in those stories, and who didn't want to be a hero? I never took into consideration that most of the heroes died in the end.

Fighting Back

In school, being that I was shy and believing that I was less-than, I never felt right around people. I was usually the second tallest person in line, and when we formed lines, we formed from shortest to tallest.

We had your typical bastards at school; the bullies, the ball-breakers. Most of the time, I took the mistreatment because I knew that as soon as an opportunity presented itself, I could run off and avoid them. On a couple of occasions when I found myself cornered, however, I fought.

My most memorable fight was in third or fourth grade with a boy named Mohammed. One day Mohammed decided it was 'Screw-with-Richard' day. The school was around the corner from my house, so Mohammed and I would often run into each other on the way to school. This particular day, Mohammed harassed me all the way there. He started bothering me during school, as well. At one point, he told me, "When we get out of school, I'm going to kick your ass."

There was a spot not far from the school and my house, and that's where he said he was going to get me. We had to wear these white aprons in school, and there was a rule that you couldn't fight with the white aprons on or you would be suspended. So, when the school day ended, I left for home.

But Mohammed wasn't done. He began to squawk like he was a big rooster. I'd had enough of him, so I went home, and took off my apron. Mohammed had committed the cardinal sin: he backed me into a corner.

I went to meet him, and when he saw me, he was surprised at first. I didn't know what the hell I was going to do. I'd never had a fight in my life.

Mohammed started to get ready. I didn't know how to fight, but there was a movie that was one of my favorites, and that movie was Gentleman Jim, with Errol Flynn. The film was about the life of Jim Corbett, who was the first true pugilistic boxer. So, I said to myself, *I don't know what the hell I'm going to do, but I'm going to practice what he did in the movie.*

I raised my fists and got in the position as Mohammed came at me. He was cocky, but before he could hit me, I jabbed him one on the face. That surprised him, and he stumbled back. Then he came at me again, and I did the same thing. Then Mohammed tried to come from underneath, but I beat him to it and hooked him from underneath. Three times was enough for him, and suddenly he thought he heard his mommy calling and ran like a coward.

My cousins were patting me on the back and telling me how great I was, but I was scared witless when I was going through that.

After this, I became increasingly self-assured, and one day I chose to get into a fight with someone from another neighborhood. I fought the guy and won, and I grew even cockier. The result of that was another fight with a fellow who had about fifty pounds on me, and he beat the hell out of me. But it wasn't like the fights you see on television or in the movies. Usually, it was just a few landed hits, and that was all.

In 1955, Argentina went through a revolution, and President Juan Peron was deposed. In that revolution, one or two soldiers got killed because they were standing in the wrong place, and Peron was forced into exile by the military. That was the extent of the revolution. It seems like there were 25 different political parties in Argentina at that time, but I was more concerned with where I was going to get my food for the day than the political climate.

The buildings were European style like you would see in France, Germany, Spain, and Italy. There are more modern buildings there now, but the thing that is most distasteful about Argentina today is that the good people live in cages. You have to have bars on the windows, and even if you live on the second or third floor, you have to have the balcony covered so no one can get in. It's bad in certain sections. Even in the good parts, if you are not protected, you will experience some misfortunes. From what I hear, most everybody there has had an experience of the dislikable kind.

It wasn't that way when I was growing up, but it wasn't that way in the United States, either, in those days.

Confrontations

The analogy I developed to explain character disorders and neurotics is this: a neurotic hears that the Eifel Tower was blown up and believes he is to blame. Meanwhile, the person with a character disorder, who actually blew up the Eifel Tower, thinks he was justified because the tower should not have been there in the first place.

According to Scott Peck, people with a character disorder almost never recover. While the neurotic assumes an inappropriate amount of responsibility, individuals with a character disorder don't assume any responsibility.

When I heard this, and knowing then that I was a person with a character disorder, I decided at that moment to become a neurotic. Even in regard to the rapes I had experienced at five and eight. I now decided I had something to do with it.

With the teenager, it was because I had wanted a ride on his bicycle. I didn't own one, and I didn't know how to ride one, and it looked like so much fun. With my uncle, I accepted responsibility because I was the one who wanted to watch him cut leather for shoes. I had now gone from one extreme to the other. I assumed full responsibility for *everything*.

Part of my problem growing up was that I could understand getting molested by the teenager – he was a stranger, I didn't know him, and I never really saw him or played with him before – but I couldn't understand what had happened with my uncle.

After my realization, I came to know that I had nothing to do with either one. I was a child.

All of these were things I needed to outgrow and come to reality with. I'm one of the few people I know that have recovered from that particular trauma, but it wasn't easy, and the process of finally coming to an understanding was two-fold.

The first step was to confront my uncle. So, I called and told him what a miserable life I'd had as a result of what he did to me. I told him about the ways in which I had struggled, and the pain I felt. I had also heard from a cousin that his step-son had committed suicide, so I told him I hoped he didn't have anything to do with the death of his stepson.

And do you know what he said throughout all of this?

Nothing.

After I finished dumping on him, I hung up the phone and went outside. I looked to the sky, and I talked to GOD. But I still had an empty feeling inside. I felt I needed to call him back.

So, I went in and called him a second time. And this time I told him, "I don't know what has happened in your life, but if you need someone to talk to, give me a call."

When I hung up the phone, I was free.

After that, whenever I would share my story, I would say that I was free of those feelings. But every time I said it, there was something inside me that would whisper, **No, you're not**.

At that time, I had a girlfriend who was into NLP: **Neuro-Linguistic Programming**. She suggested I give it a try, so I agreed.

I sat with her, and she asked me to close my eyes. Then she began by asking which of the two molestations bothered me the most. Right away I said it was the time with my uncle when I was eight. But that didn't feel correct, and I knew then that it was the first one. With my eyes still closed, I told her this.

I'm not an expert on NLP, so I can't go into much detail, but what I remember is that she began a process which diminished and ridiculized the experience with techniques such as speeding up the circumstances, minimizing the event, and making the incident into a kind of cartoon or caricature. By the time we were through, I was clear of those events. I've been clear ever since.

It is so important for me to confront my fears. As I developed, I made a practice of this.

Prior to my development, I had discovered that the same thing which happened to me had happened to a friend. The man who had molested this friend lived in New York, so I flew to New York to break this person's knees, or worse.

For a week I would go to the house and wait for him, but I could never catch him outside. So finally, I came back to Dallas. Later, after I began my development, I thought about this situation.

The reality of it was that I would go to the house, park my car across the street for a few minutes, and then I would leave. There was never any serious attempt to confront this individual.

Once I entered development, and I began to see things better, I asked my friend if he wanted to go with me to confront this man. He chose to go with me, and we confronted the man in the proper way. And thankfully for my friend, he didn't have to wait as long as I did to get well.

If I have something that needs to be confronted, that means there's an area of my life that needs improvement, and anything I confront will be beneficial to me. I can't grow from the pains I continue to experience.

Quite often I couldn't confront someone else's difficulties until I had faced my own. I used to be so secretive about my life that I had no life. The only reason I can do now what I couldn't do then is that I'm no longer isolated, from GOD, or from people. I have a spiritual advisor I talk to weekly, sometimes more or less often, depending on how things are going. I also have many wonderful people in my life, with whom I share life, and share myself. But I had to confront my difficulties for that to happen.

In the beginning, I couldn't confront them. Do you know why?

Because I was alone, and I was emotionally broken by my ideas about life.

It's Not What It Is

Even when I was able to express myself at the time, I could only do so from the level at which I saw things, which, for the most part, wasn't very good.

The desire to eliminate my anger and rage came from the growth in my understanding. I realized my anger was a demonstration of my ignorance, and how many people want to show their ignorance?

Now, suppressing it is better than exploding, but the problem with suppression is it works very well *until it doesn't*. When suppression fails, an explosion will occur. The key is to get rid of the anger, rather than suppress it.

Anything I keep, I get to keep. Anything I want to hang onto, I get to hang onto, and suffer with, if I haven't learned how to get rid of it. Suffer, and worry, and fret. Like the molestation by my uncle. But it doesn't even have to be something that severe, because we each respond in accordance with our level of reality and our understanding.

However, the reverse is true, as well. Anything I want to give up, I can give up, and suffer no more. . . when I develop the proper tools to do so.

We have a choice.

From the early beginnings of this process, I began to look for the similarities in other people, rather than the differences. I've found I can relate to almost anything, even if I have no experience with it because I can associate one thing to the other. I've never been obsessed with alcohol, but I've been obsessed with sex. I've been obsessed with control.

So it's not what it is, it's what I do with it.

One of the things I've come to know from my studies, is eventually I begin to see myself in everyone I meet.

(How is it that in my teenage years, I would go to a dance and it seemed like I was glued to a wall? As much as I wanted to ask a girl to dance or talk to one, I was just glued to that wall. My mind would be talking to me like if I approach her something was going to kill me. From where did all of these inferiorities come to me?)

Chapter 4

Humility

Not long after I began the process of clearing out the junk, I started hearing references to **humility**. I would show up to meetings in the Porsche, but as I began to hear more about humility, I started to ask myself, "Richard, how can you be humble in a brand-new Porsche 928?"

Although I was beginning to learn about this principle, I still had no comprehension of the word **humility**.

One of the things I sometimes heard was that humility is the ability to be humble, but this definition provided nothing for me. So the first thing I needed to do was develop a proper concept and understanding of this principle.

Simply stated, **humility is the ability to see things as they are.** Not how I would like them to be. Not how I *feel* them to be. Simply as they are.

Besides the problem with trying to be humble in a Porsche, I still had the $1050 a month car payment, and only $3500 to my name. So, among all the other things I had to let go on my journey, I realized the car had to go as well.

I decided to return the car to the dealer. As I drove down the freeway, the true meaning of humility came to me. It was the ability to see things as they were, not as I wished them to be. It was the opposite of arrogance.

When I got to the dealership, I walked in and handed them the keys.

"I can't pay for this vehicle anymore," I said. "Goodbye."

And that was the end of the Porsche.

Returning it was a humbling experience. It wasn't that I became humble because of it, but I at least had more of a sense of humility than I did before. And I finally began to understand the word and the concept behind it.

After my ex-wife and I went our separate ways, I divorced her. But the truth is I didn't divorce her because I didn't love her. I divorced her because, for the first time, I began to see what real love in a relationship should be, and I didn't have that for her.

After the divorce, however, there were some large debts to pay. Over $50,000 in all, but I paid them. For a while, I worked at Just Brakes. For some time after that, I was a management consultant traveling across the country. It took ten or eleven years, but I paid my debts, and I paid them by being a worker.

Leaving the business to my ex-wife wasn't a smart thing to do. She was unable to manage an operation of that size, and it went under within a year.

Once I started to realize my mind was such a problem, I would notice people making statements such as, "My mind is like a bad neighborhood. I try not to go there alone."

I've mentioned moving from one level of reality to another, and this is an example of that principle. When I believed those things as well, I was at a lower level of reality. But then remembered what I had heard about the thinking mind, and I thought, ***Wait a minute. . . My mind is supposed to be working for me. I can't have it working for me if I think it's my enemy.***

It occurred to me that I needed to befriend my mind. With this thought, I moved to a different level of reality. I understood what was happening and made a decision to change my thinking.

Habits and Choices

A lot of the problems I had experienced were a result of the barriers and beliefs I had created for myself. I started to understand a little about the subconscious, and I learned that the subconscious doesn't joke around.

Whatever I say, **my subconscious takes literally**. Therefore, I'm careful with what I say.

Take restless sleep for example. Say I wake up a couple of times during the night. And say this happens on more than one occasion. If I begin to think that this is something I do, and I begin to tell myself, *Oh, this is normal for me, I simply don't sleep well*, then I have created a habit. And since I have thought it, and perhaps spoken it aloud to someone, my subconscious now believes that this is something I do. I have therefore perpetuated a habit of waking up in the middle of the night.

Instead, I must become conscious of what I am affirming, and tell myself, *It's not that I wake up every three hours now. It was just a couple of times.*

I can further correct the narrative by telling myself that I always sleep well at night, and by thanking GOD for my deep and restful sleep.

Since my subconscious takes things literally, I must be mindful of what I feed it. This is something I'm very aware of today.

Once in a while, my mind will give me an insane thought. While this seldom occurs now, it used to happen continually. Though I can't control what comes into my mind, ***I can choose how long it remains there***. That's what I started to practice: choosing not to go with a thought, or to change it, or to discard it altogether, without any ill feelings on the matter.

I don't argue with my thoughts. I simply assess them and address or dismiss them as necessary.

I don't worry when I have an intrusive thought. I don't wonder where it came from, what I should do about it, and I don't beat myself up for still thinking that way. What I do instead is look at the reality of the situation. What has occurred here?

I had an insane thought. That's all.
That was it?
Yes.

Good.

My mind is a part of me, just like my arms, just like my legs. They are to serve me, not destroy me like they used to do. They are to do as I determine, and aid in my development and in helping me live happily. I am not my mind. My mind is a part of me. So it's not about protecting my mind, it's about protecting myself.

In the beginning, what I needed the most was to see those things through the eyes of the people who were guiding me. That is one reason having a mentor is so critical. My mentors offered a perspective on my reality that I wasn't capable of achieving for myself. They helped me to see things the way they were, unfiltered by my emotions and misthinking.

It's like school. To teach a subject to a class, there has to be a teacher. It's the same thing with developing a good life. I call this the jungle of life. If I'm going to go through the jungles of Africa, I would find a guide. I wouldn't go kicking around the bushes by myself. It's the same way with developing an understanding of myself and the world.

I used to feel so much less-than inside of me, but I didn't understand these feelings, even though I was acting on them daily. Most people don't know what they don't know, and I was in that boat, ignorant of what I was feeling and why.

Developing humility was almost the same as when I first exposed my molestations. I have often called them molestations, but that's really too nice of a word because they were rapes. I couldn't expose those rapes, and call them for what they were, because it would have made a messed-up person like me even more messed-up to use the word.

One result of those two incidents, which I didn't even understand until much later, was a severe internal confusion. I didn't know if I was a man, woman, or what. I knew I wasn't a woman because I had the wrong equipment. I knew I liked women and desired them, and I didn't feel any attraction towards men. And yet, I didn't feel like a man.

So what am I?

My confusion lay in this: I could understand one person doing that to me, but why two? Did I have something to do with it? Was it something within me that others could see?

I had developed a lot of erroneous beliefs as a result. The realization that I had met up with the most ignorant man in the world, and that it was me, was a blessing, and it was only by the grace of GOD that I came to that realization.

In essence, they helped me develop humility.

I began to see how my own intelligence, up to that point, had done nothing but ruin my life. It had done so with insecurities, shortcomings, lack of trust, and unhappiness; the distortion of all things. Upon realizing this, I began to see my own intelligence as an Achilles' heel, and when I started to see it as such, it began to be real intelligence.

In other words, what I needed to do in the beginning was to stop listening to me, so that I could begin to hear.

One of the understandings that I came to see was that in order to have happiness, I needed to learn to practice happiness. The best way for me to practice happiness is *being grateful for all things.*

Today, *my life is not my happiness. My happiness is my life.*

Grace

In the beginning, I became so filled with a sense of GOD that I actually began to step away from reality. If I had been in reality, and aware, I would have never given the business to someone who didn't know how to manage it.

Through my studies, I began to work my way toward finding balance. I had learned the value of study as a child, and so, for the first ten to twenty years of my development, I studied and read a lot. As a result, I became more prolific in developing a good life, and living a good life. I utilized these other sources of knowledge as mentors, also. I treated them as textbooks and began to practice what was outlined.

For example, it occurred to me one day, at that time, that I didn't know how to smile. I turned to GOD, as I had learned to do since first feeling his presence on the drive to Hazelden, and I began to pray, *GOD, please teach me how to smile.*

I prayed this prayer every morning for a year and a half, but guess what. . . I wasn't smiling.

During this time of intense research, I made a habit of listening to someone speak who wasn't me. Often, I did this in the car, or with a portable cassette player and a pair of headphones. And when I found a cassette or series that was beneficial, I would listen to it repeatedly, sometimes 30, 40, perhaps even 50 times, and I wouldn't move on to the next cassette until I had thoroughly researched and studied the contents, and knew everything the speaker was going to say before he said it.

So one day I was listening to a tape by a life mentor when he began to paraphrase the Bible. What he said was, "How are you going to believe you got something that you ain't got? Well, you've got to know that every precious gift was given at the foundation of the earth, and it's the Father's good pleasure to give you His kingdom."

I had listened to this particular tape 20 or 30 times before, but this was the first time I was ready to receive this message, and my prayer changed that day. Instead of, **GOD, please teach me how to smile**, I began thanking GOD.

GOD, thank you for having taught me to smile.

I've come to see since that moment that most of the time I've spent waiting on GOD, GOD was waiting on me. Soon after I began thanking GOD for what I believed I already possessed, I began to smile.

One of my first jobs after leaving the business was a consulting gig, but this involved a lot of cold-calling, which I hated with a passion. Each call was agony to suffer through, and I did so, day after day, call after call. After a few successes, I knew I had the ability, and this became my justification for continuing on, but eventually, I had to make a decision.

So I said to myself, ***I'm able to do it, but I still dislike the hell out of it, so I'm not doing it anymore.***

Despite this experience, my positivity continued to grow. This was when I went to work at Just Brakes, and by then I was an incredibly positive person. I had eliminated a number of things from my life and had learned to use the power of positive thinking to keep myself well. I had also found a sense of grace and freedom I had never known before.

But as essential as positivity is, it has its limits. The incident which revealed this to me was when I came down with pneumonia. I had been talking myself out of being sick, but pneumonia had nothing to do with what I was telling myself. I couldn't stop coughing and even cracked a couple of ribs doing so.

When I finally went to the doctor, and he told me what I had, I finally realized there was a limit to positivity. I still practice positive thinking, but since that time I've developed a useful guideline when it comes to not feeling well.

The first day, I use positive thinking. The second day, I call the doctor.

This has worked a whole lot better.

Along with positive thinking, I developed another habit which has been crucial to living in a state of peace and happiness. That habit is gratitude.

I'm grateful for all things. I'm grateful for all experiences. And I'm grateful for my willingness.

But, I only got here by the grace of GOD. I never understood what it meant to live in a state of grace until I looked up the definition of the word grace.

Grace is a free gift.

I started to wonder how this was applicable to my life. What determines whether or not I live in a state of grace?

The analogy I developed was this: One of the cars I've loved the most was my Porsche 928. So I said to myself, let's make believe grace is a Porsche 928, and let's make believe it's parked in the garage. What would happen if every day, instead of jumping in my Porsche, I go out the front door, walking, or crawling, or, at best, riding a bike.

While I'm walking, grace remains in the garage. It takes me much longer to get where I'm going. I might begin to get frustrated wondering why life is so hard. And the reality is that the solution is right here, if I choose to use it.

With this analogy, I realized there was a state of grace available to me that I wasn't utilizing. I must always remember: even though grace is a free gift, unless I use it, it has no value.

Now, when most people hear that we live in a state of grace, it doesn't mean anything to them. The word spirituality is thrown around so often these days that they have no working definition or how to practically apply it in their lives. I didn't know that spirituality gives life to the physical. I didn't know it's the highest form of reality.

These are words people take for granted. They are so powerful, and so incredible, and yet people seldom look into them, just like I used to do.

How about grace?

And understanding?

And will?

Powerful words, and powerful concepts. They are available to anyone who will accept them. The Porsche is in the garage, and the keys are on the table.

I just have to make the choice to drive it, that is to say, to *use* grace.

To *live* in grace, I must *use* it.

Miracles

One of the primary ways I've developed is in my understanding of GOD, and my appreciation for the miracles I've experienced.

I see many people, both religious and non-religious, that are looking for the burning bush. I've had many burning bushes in my life, and none of them were burning bushes. Furthermore, many of the miracles I received, in my old ignorance, I attributed afterward to luck.

In my early twenties, I worked at a factory. There was a particular piece of equipment there, a grinder, which weighed six or seven hundred pounds. Occasionally, while grinding a product, the machine would get jammed. When this happened, we would raise it with a forklift, remove the obstruction, and then lower the grinder back into the hole in which it sat. There was a connecting piece about a foot round, which, upon clearing the jam, would have to be realigned.

I was working alone one day when a jam occurred. After raising the machine with a forklift, and clearing the jam, I went to realign the connecting piece. As I did, I placed my hand between the upper portion and the floor.

The moment I did this, I realized it wasn't a smart thing to do, and the moment I had that realization, the piece of equipment dropped into the hole. . . with my four fingers in between.

I had been around equipment like this since I was nine years old, and I knew better than to make such a foolish mistake. I also knew what this meant for me. You could often see men at plants like this with missing digits, missing hands, missing limbs. There was a heavy price to pay for carelessness.

My thoughts raced.

I just cut off my four fricking fingers, GOD, please don't let it happen, Richard, how can you be so fricking stupid, you just cut off your four fricking fingers, GOD, please, don't let it happen!

By this time a fellow by the name of Ochoa had arrived. Ochoa moved quickly and used the forklift to raise the piece of equipment. I brought my hand out, fully expecting to be minus four fingers, but when I looked all I could see was a trace across the tops.

My fingers are all here, I thought. ***But they're not supposed to be.***

I went to the emergency room, expecting that since they hadn't been amputated, they must at least be broken. After examining the x-rays, however, the doctor told me that the bones were fine. My only injuries were lacerations.

My next thought was, **GOD, I'm lucky.**

I forgot all about my prayer.

Since the day I was told I had a room ready at Hazelden, I began to develop a relationship with GOD. I started to look at aspects of my life differently.

Looking back on this incident, and others of similar magnitude, I realized that GOD had been taking care of me. I could then determine that he would **always** take care of me.

To this day, that faith, reliance, and trust continue to grow.

Now, even though I speak of this faith, reliance, and trust I have in GOD, it's important to understand that it doesn't have to be any different for a person who doesn't believe in GOD. This sense of peace can be achieved by that person, as well, albeit with a different understanding, if they so choose.

Just like with grace, positivity, and gratitude, we have a choice. The only thing that was required of me was to cease behaving as if **I** were GOD.

When I was five-and-a-half, my mother would drop me off at school, and I would immediately run away. By the time she returned to the house, I was already there. After struggling with this for a while, she stopped taking me altogether, deciding that perhaps it was best if I start the following year. I didn't have to begin school again until I was six-and-a-half, at least.

I would like to tell you it was because I was such a rebel. I used to think of myself as a rebel, a rule-breaker, a person in charge of his own destiny. In retrospect, however, it was because I was already living in **extreme fear**. I couldn't be left alone with anyone else.

I also used to consider myself independent. But when I began to examine my independence, I came to the realization that everything controlled me. Money controlled me. Traffic controlled me. The cashier at the checkout controlled me. Anything at all had the power to take away my good emotions. That does not demonstrate independence.

Today I'm independent because all of those things, a vast majority of the time, have no power over me.

But to develop in this way, I needed to realize what my intelligence was demonstrating. For the first 37 years of my life, my intelligence demonstrated that I wasn't very intelligent. I was actually ignorant, foolish, and quite often stupid.

Today I live in peace and freedom. Nothing has the power to control me. Sometimes things affect me, but only for a brief moment. GOD has given me my arms and legs to work for me. My hands and feet, to work for me.

And my mind, to work for me.

Not so I can work for it.

I'll tell you how I arrived at this understanding. It was by looking at all the many miracles I've experienced throughout my life. For instance, a person who barely graduated from primary school should never have been able to accomplish the things I've accomplished. And yet, I have accomplished many wonderful things. The most wonderful thing I have accomplished is my development through GOD's grace.

I have not been happy and joyful for over thirty-two years now, but for over thirty-two years, most of the time, I have been peaceful, I have been secure, and I have been tranquil, even in the middle of many difficult situations, such as going from rich to poor, divorce, problematic relationships, and much more.

In all that time I've had one bad day. One! And when I say it was a bad day, what I mean is I had more negative experiences happen that day than positive. All of the other days I've had bad moments, but not bad days because there is always something to be grateful for, something to appreciate, and a reason to thank GOD for the wonderful life we live.

And that's a miracle in itself.

Manifestations

There's a verse in the Bible where ol' Job says, "What I feared has come upon me; what I dreaded has happened to me."

Did Job expect catastrophe?

Did he worry about it and dwell on it?

Did he think it in his heart, and so it was?

What I believe, what I think in my heart, has a way of manifesting in my life. If I think positive things, and dwell on positive things, I more frequently receive positive things. But it works the other way, as well. If I dwell on negativity, and dissatisfaction, and complaints, then I receive more of those, as well. That's also the way I've destroyed many of my relationships; by thinking negatively about them, and dwelling on things that didn't matter.

This is why it is so important that I watch what I say and think. Whatever I speak into my life, tends to appear in my life, in one way or another. Any thought that I devote a lot of attention to is a prayer for something to happen or to not happen. I can devote attention to something negative with worry and anxiety and actually create the thing I was worried about or afraid of.

Whenever I'm not feeling well, I don't dwell on it, or talk too much about it. What I do instead is pray, and the way I pray is like this.

"GOD, thank you for having healed me."

I don't know how GOD does it, but He does. Always.

Oh. . . As a man thinks it in his heart, so is it.

When thinking about the future, people often construct more misery than is available. Their thoughts and minds are filled with trepidation, and the unfortunate thing is that by focusing on these things they are actually drawing them nearer, calling them into their lives.

On the other hand, many successful people (some famous ones, as well) will tell you that they visualized their success long before it ever occurred. They constructed the life they wanted in their mind and in their heart, and they meditated on these desires. It did not come instantly, and as with the spiritual principle of what you sow you reap, it doesn't always happen exactly the way it was envisioned. But, the belief was key. Dwelling on what they wanted, rather than what they didn't want, was essential. Another way this operates is 'whether I think of myself as a success or failure, I am correct.'

I've mentioned the first time I heard the phrase, ***"The thinking mind is a wonderful servant, or a horrible master,"*** and how that understanding stopped me in my tracks. That was when I considered the possibility that I was supposed to be directing my mind.

The more I have studied on this subject, the more I've come to see that I need to make my mind an employee of mine, rather than me being bossed around by my mind like it did for the first 37 plus years.

Mankind has done some magnificent things when we have put our minds to work for us. Flight, computers, the moon landing.

Before any of these could manifest in the world, they required thought, and mental construction, and the belief that it could be done. For instance, I wouldn't start building a house without first creating the blueprints, and that principles remains true in all areas of life.

We have these incredible minds at our disposal, capable of thinking, and feeling, and believing. And what we believe we call forth, we draw near, we manifest.

When I put my mind to work for me, rather than the other way around, and I believed in my heart what I wished to see in my life, I was finally able to stop sabotaging myself as I used to do.

I came to understand that GOD has never done anything negative or derogative to me. He has never given me troubles or difficulties.

All of those were created by me, and by a mind that had been negatively influenced by the society in which it had developed. GOD gives me the power not only to overcome the difficulties I've created for myself but to manage my mind so as to prevent creating new difficulties in my future. GOD gave me brains, and he gave me them to use. If I don't utilize them properly, it's like the Porsche sitting in the garage while I walk around.

The reason my molestations were so devastating to me was that I kept them a secret, which in turn created a lot of irrational fears. These secrets, and the subsequent fears, changed my experience of reality and gave me a lot of negativity to dwell upon, which in turn called more negativity into my life.

When I realized the answer was to expose my secrets, and I began to do so freely, I also exposed the fears for what they were; irrational. I have been free of those secrets and the fears they created for nearly 30 years, and I no longer lack a sense of being whole.

I began to live in positivity, and more positivity began to manifest.

But first I had to believe.

(How is it that for years I was in an eternal conversation about nothing? And 90% of the conversations that I thought about never happened. Although I'm saying 90%, it could've been 99%, because I couldn't remember any of those conversations afterwards anyhow. But they sure were bothering me!)

Chapter 5

The Thinking Mind. . .

How is it that I needed to wait until I was 37 years old to begin to see that my mind was supposed to be working for me? How is it that my own mind had been terrorizing me for 37 years. . . and I didn't even know it!

I thought my life was normal. All the stress, and anger, and rage, and misery. That was just the normal way to be, wasn't it?

No one ever told me that my mind was a tool. Not my parents, not my teachers, not my aunts or uncles or cousins or friends. No one told me this, because they didn't know it, either.

The mind is a tool, and a supremely powerful one, at that. I didn't go to school for a great deal of time, but I've come to see since then that even college graduates know as little about this principle as I did at that time.

I began to ask myself, *"is my mind me, or is it supposed to be working for me?"*

I didn't know, so I began researching, and studying, and meditating on the subject. The answer I came to was this.

Many times, throughout my life, my mind has told me to do some insane, crazy, stupid things, and I didn't do them. On the same token, there have been times when my mind has told me to do something good, or helpful, or beneficial, and I didn't do those things, either.

But how could that be the case?

So then I asked where do these thoughts come fromt? How was my mind working?

I started to see that my mind was operating from within my inhibitions, my shortcomings, my sense of not having enough, of lack, insecurity, and inferiority.

I was operating, I realized, from society, and all the things I had inadvertently been taught by society. I was being what society had shown me I should be. I was acting the way society showed me I should act. That was even crazier.

When I first discovered this, I was still in the furniture business. I was blessed to know at that point, since I was a rich man, that I didn't have to continue pursuing happiness through wealth. I had already achieved a measure of wealth and had discovered no happiness there.

I needed to find something within myself that would produce the type of freedom I always wanted to possess, the kind of independence I always desired.

When I saw that my mind had been doing more harm than good, I began to ask myself, "would GOD give me something that would be of detriment to me?"

At that moment, I began to look at my mind differently.

If I could do something that my mind told me not to do, or the opposite, that meant I had some choice in the matter. That led to the realization that there is something beyond the mind, some mechanism operating below the surface that I couldn't see and didn't understand. Then, I began to learn about the subconscious.

One of the things I learned was that until I bring consciousness into my life, I am ruled by the subconscious. One of the ways in which I am ruled is automatic or near-automatic responses to anything that happens to me.

If I was driving down the highway and another car cut me off, I would have an automatic reaction; rage.

When I thought of myself as an independent person, and someone told me what to do or how to do it, I would have an automatic reaction; rebellion.

If I wanted something, and for some reason, I couldn't have it, I would have an automatic reaction; depression.

I had been governed by a secret part of my mind that I didn't know existed. Until I understood this and began to develop consciousness, I had little control over my reactions.

I used to smoke cigarettes. In the beginning, I smoked because I was trying to show that I was tough, or cool, or macho, but as I progressed in my habit, the subconscious took over. At that point, I would light up on cue. For example, whenever I finished eating, while I was having a coke, after sex, or if I was bored. There were flags telling me when and where to have a cigarette, and these flags weren't even visible to me. I was living in automatic mode, and not just with smoking, either. With my feelings, with my reactions, with everything!

Knowing this, I could see things in a more positive way. The more I removed the negativity from my head, and replaced it with positivity, the better I felt. The more I learned to slow my thoughts down and think in a more deliberate, conscious manner, the better my life became.

I also needed to understand why my mind was like this in the first place, so I began to search out the origins of my negativity and automatic reactions.

Insanity in Society

No one ever told me I was supposed to be managing my mind. I didn't know this as a child, or as a teenager, or for most of my early adult life. Therefore, my mind, when left unattended, had assimilated with all of the drawbacks, insecurities, and inferiorities that society had to offer. Has that been your experience?

I was always too much of one thing or too little of another. Someone else always had more than me, and to compare or compete, I needed to have as much (or more) than they did. All of this contributed to a cycle of fear and insecurity, and that is how I lived my life; in fear and insecurity.

Thus, it was important for me to realize the insanity of society, and subsequently, the way my mind was operating as a result of that influence.

I used to believe that my thinking was terrible. The way I thought, to a large extent and on a daily basis, was troublesome. My own mind was always bothering me. And what it told me was always the same: I needed more, and it was never enough, and the more I got, the more it wasn't enough.

I began to see that thinking is for constructing, and what I was doing was not constructing. So the problem wasn't necessarily with my thinking, it was with my misthinking. I had the right tool, but I was using it in the wrong way.

Why?

Because every message from society I had ever received, every influence society had sent my way, had told me that this was normal, and this was the way to be.

Society excels at one thing in particular, and that is in the promotion of negative thoughts and behaviors. When I became deranged at the age of 37, I was not sleeping very much. A few hours here, a few hours there. At times, to justify my insanity, I would say the reason I slept so little was because I was so much more intelligent than everyone else. I didn't need as much sleep as they did, and if I slept less, I could get more done.

Society tells us that's a good thing. I was working harder than everyone else. I was accomplishing and acquiring more than everyone else. That was the goal, wasn't it? More, more, more.

The same with my racing, rapid-fire thoughts. My thoughts were always going 200 miles-per-hour. But that just meant I could process more information, come up with better ideas, and outsmart the competition, right? It even helped with sleeping less, because I had such a commotion going on in my head that I could only sleep for a few hours at a time anyway.

This was how society had encouraged me to be, and I couldn't even see the insanity of it.

When I finally came to see this reality, I realized I needed to learn how to sleep. This may sound odd, but the first time I slept adequately was when, right before I went to sleep, I prayed, "GOD, I turn my sleep over to your care."

I slept over eight hours, and I've hardly ever interfered with my sleep since.

It was the same with my thoughts. I had to learn how to slow down my thoughts.

The more I began to utilize my mind, the better my life became. But I first had to see how my mind had assimilated with the insanity of society, and how that societal mind had filled me with inadequacies, shame, guilt, and fear.

As a result of taking charge of my mind, my life has become something I could never dream of. I never knew this kind of life was possible, this beautiful life of tranquility, peace, and peace of mind. I never knew this could exist.

But before I could arrive here, I had to realize that the mind I have is mine to use, not for me to be used by it. No one ever taught me that. I never heard that. And I believe that is something that needs to be taught to our children, and to grownups alike.

To banish my unmanageability, and the unmanageability of my mind, I had to turn my cares over to GOD. I also learned how to appreciate the miracles in each day. Most important, I started to understand how the insanity of society had prevented me from operating in positiveness.

When my mind calls me and sends me into fear, the mind of society is in charge of me. The trick is to recognize when that mind of society is calling upon me, and to realize that this mind of society provides me with nothing a vast majority of the time. Then, the key is to replace negative thoughts with positive thoughts.

Generational Insanity

Nobody ever told me my mind was supposed to be working for me. And I never saw anyone utilize their mind in that way, either. Everywhere I looked I saw people with a lot of anger in them. Anger, and negativity, and, as a result, unhappiness. I seldom saw anyone who had developed poise and balance.

Sober, if you will, which is defined as balance.

As I began to recognize that the mind which was always bothering me was not my own, but that of society, I began systematically to change my thoughts. Revising the way I thought led to a shift in the way my mind operated. Being positive became something I did subconsciously, as an automatic response, just as being negative had been prior.

When I let go of the mind society had inculcated in me, the mind of GOD began to manifest. The more that mind manifested, the better my wellbeing became.

I came to see that there was a problem with generational insanity, and that problem was this; each generation picks up the previous generations screwups. When I began to take a look at my issues and had the talk with my mother about her childhood, I saw four more generations of negativity, imbalance, and insanity. When my son looks at his problems, he probably sees five or six generations of the same.

When I have an imbalance, I do not possess stability. Whether something is all the way to the left or the right, I'm going to get the same result. Being sober means being balanced. It means being of sound mind and living in consciousness.

It's easy for parents to give out amusements. Whether that's television, smartphones, or video games, if there is no balance, no sobriety, the result will be the same. When the children become spoiled, many parents perpetuate a cycle of concession, resulting in the absence of gratefulness, which is one of the most potent tools in ridding oneself of negativity.

Too often, as parents, we fail to teach gratitude.

When I wanted to learn how to be happy, I had to learn to be consciously grateful for all the wonderful things that had been – and continue to be – given to me. I don't count what I have, or compare what I have with what others have. I simply thank GOD for all He has done, does, and will continue to do.

If we want to curtail the insanity passed down from generation to generation, we must teach our children the same.

The Molded Mind

From the moment I started breathing (I can't say living, because that didn't occur until the age of 37), every experience that had happened was molding my mind.

Whether it was being afraid of people who were bigger than me, or people who raised their voice, or people who tried to shame and bully me. All of that created a repertoire for my mind, and being that I didn't know I was supposed to be in charge, my mind molded itself around everything that was negative in my life.

Anytime I react to something, consciously or unconsciously, I'm responding to some experience in my past. Often that past experience has nothing to do with the present moment.

When I was five or six, my cousin had a dog. The dog was a Terrier, and as a prank (or perhaps to be cruel), my cousin set the dog after me. The dog chased me, barking and biting, until my mother ran it off with a broom.

After that, I was always afraid of dogs.

When my mother and father split up, I began to suffer from feelings of inadequacy. I felt less-than. We started living in terms of lack and want, and like the dog, those experiences molded my mind.

It wasn't until I began learning how to develop a life, and heard the phrase, "The thinking mind is a wonderful servant, or a horrible master," that I began working toward managing my mind.

Early in my development, when I heard something crazy come into my head, I would think, **Where the hell did that thought come from?**

Then I would send it away.

Though that may sound odd, in the beginning, I needed to separate myself from that mind, because it was harmful. At times I would even say to my own thoughts, **You're** *crazy, get away from me*, as if I was separate from them.

I needed to replace my negative thoughts with positive thoughts. And the more I did that, the better my life became.

Good things are just like bad things in this sense: Whatever I persist upon the most is what I will succeed with. I persisted with replacing negative thoughts with positive ones, and I began to succeed. After a while, I became the most positive person I knew.

I was still not wholly positive, but it was no longer a fight. And whenever a negative thought appears today, I merely say, *Really? After all this time?*

One of the things that also helped me was when I realized that I didn't know how to be happy. Just like humility and will and willingness and the other words I hadn't fully understood, the first thing I needed to do to learn how to be happy was to look up the word and find out exactly what it meant.

So I looked up happy in the dictionary, and the first thing I read was *a heavenly state*. I understood this as my connection to GOD, and my most precious moments were those in which I was connecting to the GOD of my understanding and beliefs.

Understanding was also a keyword for me, so I began to explore that and to ask myself what it meant to have an understanding or misunderstanding.

When I had an understanding, I was alright. When I had a misunderstanding, I was running all over the place. A misunderstanding meant a lack of security. I couldn't be secure in whatever knowledge or lack of knowledge I possessed at that moment. It was not a good feeling.

One of the things I did early on was to study things that were meaningful and valuable and compare them to the things I was still doing that were not meaningful or of any value. I would meditate on these things, and at the end of the meditation, I would make decisions on how to behave differently.

What I've seen in many people is when they do read things, they may say, Yeah, that was wonderful, but then continue on without making a decision to be different. Subsequently, each time they have a new realization, it's about an old realization that they didn't do anything about the first time.

A lot of the errors I committed in life were habitual. It wasn't that I made a million different mistakes, it was that I made the same few over and over and over again.

In the very beginning, I made the same errors most people make. The only difference is that since my development, I've stopped making them repeatedly.

When I make a mistake these days, I often ask myself, ***How is it that I did that? I know better than this.***

But then I correct myself and check with someone who has developed a better life than me.

Realizations continue all the time and development never ceases.

Meditation

Quite often when people refer to meditation, what they are actually talking about is going into a trance; in other words, ***shutting down the mind***. When I go into trance, it's only for brief moments, and one of the things I do in those moments is listen to my heart. That's when I empty my mind of all thoughts, which, in my own case, is not something I'm able to do for any length of time. Nor would I want to, even though a smile comes immediately to my face.

Why?

Because nothingness begets nothing.

At first, I meditated in a more rigorous, or continuous way, but I no longer do that. What I do instead is meditate throughout the day, all day long. These meditations typically last for only a few seconds at a time, and rather than trance, involve consciousness. When I meditate in this way, I am aware of what is going on in me and around me, but not in a way in which is difficult, or feels like work. The way I do it is very freeing for me.

I began to find relief from worry and stress when I came to the realization that GOD had always been taking care of me, is taking care of me, and will continue to take care of me. I believe He does this for anyone who begins to develop this belief.

This was something I had to learn to be in tune with. It was not that GOD came from above and said, "You're safe!" It was a process of developing understanding and realizing that (for too long) the only gods I had in my life were people, places, and things. And most of them were attached to my limitations rather than empowering me.

The way I used my meditation in the beginning was I started to study things that allowed me to develop a reality about myself and the world around me. Every time I recognized a behavior in myself that was derogatory, or a belief within me that was negative and harmful, I meditated upon ways to improve these aspects of my life. My meditation in this regard would lead to a decision about how to remove those thoughts and behaviors.

This belief is no longer my belief.

This type of behavior, I no longer practice.

Was I successful every time from the moment I first decided? No. It was a process, and I was persistent. It was that persistent process which led to eventual success, even with my more stubborn thoughts and behaviors.

About thirty years ago I dated a woman who practiced meditation as most people understand it, and she was trying to sell me on this kind of trance meditation. She made all the usual claims in regard to more peace and tranquility, but as soon as the wind blew the wrong way, *she would become deranged and insane*. I didn't consider that to be great evolvement. If I spend my morning in a trance, and yet I'm still controlled by the wind what good has that done me?

One of the first things I needed to understand was the actual meaning of the word *meditation*. The word *meditate* has nothing to do with going into a trance. *Meditate* means *to think about*.

If I see a problem and congratulate myself on recognizing the problem, but then fail to make a decision to change it, I haven't accomplished anything.

But if I see a problem and say, *This is wonderful because it means I don't need to practice that any longer. Now, what kind of decision do I choose to make?*

Then I can effect change in my life.

When that happens, I get happy because I don't have to continue being the way I was.

Most people receive the same wonderful message about the same thing many times over before they make a change. Because things by themselves don't change.

In the 1980s there were sugar packets with quotations on them, and the one about experience is one I remember quite vividly. It said experience gives us the ability to recognize when we make the same mistake over again.

What does experience provide, then?

Experience alone provides nothing. If it did, people wouldn't have to steal a thousand times or get drunk a thousand times, or cheat a thousand times before realizing how detrimental that behavior is. So experience itself provides no wisdom whatsoever.

It's the extraction of information from that experience that provides a new way of thinking and being. The great news is that we don't have to beat ourselves up over our mistakes and can even appreciate when one occurs because it is an opportunity for further refinement.

We can be happy to see our mistakes because that means they don't have to be repeated.

Becoming a Student

One thing that has been constant in my view of the world is the realization that most people don't know what they don't know. In other words, there are gaps in their knowledge and understanding, and they are unaware of these gaps. I have gaps in my understanding, but if I am aware of them, I can make an attempt to fill them. If I am unaware of the holes in my understanding, I won't make any changes to remedy that problem.

The saddest part about humankind is that we often operate in ignorance of *ourselves*. If a person does not have their own mind, they don't have themselves. Human beings in society today are controlled by their development, in whichever way that development has or has not occurred. In this society positiveness is not our greatest asset. The things that happen today, the vast majority of the time, are derogative, and they work to minimize our wellbeing rather than expand it.

The deal is to recognize this and then (whether a person believes in GOD or not) show through our actions that the mind we have is supposed to work for us.

How many times have I told myself, *I'm not doing that?* This action demonstrates that there is a mind that can be managed.

My first teacher, GOD love him, never had the life I have, and he was never truly happy. Most of his life was not anything upon which to model one's own, but what he did for me was teach me to be a student. I had to be willing, but he showed me the way to learn.

I will always love him, and he has been indispensable in my development and happiness. And this is what we need for ourselves, and our children.

We must all learn to be students, to fill the gaps in our knowledge and understanding, to meditate on our thoughts and behaviors, to make decisions to change them, and then have those decisions checked by somebody who is ahead of us.

Even to this day, I have my great ideas checked by my spiritual advisor. That way I know whether it is a great idea or not. As a result, my life is not my happiness. My happiness is my life.

(How is it that at times my mind becomes so bothersome that I want to take a vacation from it?)

Chapter 6

Faith and Love

Some say faith is as faith does. Love is as love does.

I didn't know what faith was. When I began to ask about it, I found that many people had trouble coming up with a simple answer.

The simplest answer I've found for faith is **blind trust.**

Another word that was very good for me to learn was the word confidence. Confidence has one of the same ingredients as faith. The first three letters, **con**, mean **with**. And fide means **trust**. So when I'm **confident**, I'm doing something **with trust**.

After learning this, I realized that in some areas I had a great deal of confidence, and in others, I had very little. Take dating for example. I never really pursued the women I thought I wanted. I settled for the ones who wanted me. This was due to my insecurities.

But upon realizing this, I was able to put the necessary thoughts and actions in place to develop confidence in those areas.

This is not to say I've achieved perfection. This is a process of continual growth. But one thing I have accomplished, and I almost brag about this, is that I have stopped bothering me. **No one bothered me more than me**. No one was better at finding faults and flaws with myself than I was. If another person had treated me as badly as my own mind treated me, **I would have killed him.**

The mind I possess today is a mind that provides tranquility, peacefulness, and happiness. The last time I was bothered by an obsessive thought was over a year ago, and I can't remember what it was so it couldn't have been that important. And in the last 33 years, I've only met one other person who could say the same.

He was a pastor at a church on Forest Lane. I had been experiencing difficulties with a cousin of mine. We were partners in a restaurant, and some tough decisions needed to be made. So first, I consulted with one of my spiritual advisors. He made some suggestions, but they didn't seem meaningful enough. There was another place I knew of, where they suggested I take a particular course. This was a Tuesday, and the course was on Thursday, so I thought, **Well if I don't have the answer by then I'll come back and take the course.**

So I went to the church on Forest Lane to speak with the pastor, but he wasn't available. I instead ended up talking with his wife, and by the time I left, I had a solution to my problem.

The reason I remember this so well is because the pastor used to frequent a restaurant I owned. At one point I discovered he had terminal cancer. When I next saw him, I didn't know what to say, so I simply said, "I hope everything goes well."

To which he replied, "Everything **is** well."

Death and Fear

It is always painful to lose someone we care about, but I'll tell you what I do when someone I love has passed on: I rejoice in having known them. My mother died nine years ago, and yes, I shed tears, but there was no depression.

There was a television show in the 1990s called Wings. It was a sitcom set in a small airport in Nantucket, Massachusetts, where the Hackett brothers ran an airline called Sandpiper Air. Joe and Brian were the two brothers, and they had a mechanic named Lowell who wasn't too swift.

Sitcoms, of course, are entertainment. They are meant to make us laugh. But one episode, in particular, pointed to something tremendously powerful and spiritual.

The episode, number 20 of season 4, is called, "Goodbye Old Friend,"

In this episode, the two brothers find out that Weeb Gilroy, who was very close to Lowell, has died, and they're trying to find a way to break the news to him. So, they, along with Faye, another employee of theirs, take Lowell into the office and tell him the news.

When Lowell first hears that Weeb Gilroy has passed away, he says, "No, he didn't. Weeb Gilroy's not dead," and a moment later leaves the room.

As soon as he's gone, the three begin to discuss the five stages of grief: Denial, anger, bargaining, depression, and acceptance. Lowell, it seems, is in the first stage. He's denying that Weeb is dead. And over the next few months, they ascertain, he'll go through the other four.

But no sooner have they said this when Lowell burst back into the room.

"I'm angry as hell at Weeb for dying!" he shouts. Then, calmly, he says, "But I'd trade anything to get him back. GOD, what's the use, it's hopeless. He's gone."

And then, after one more pause, he says, "But, what are you going to do? Life goes on," and leaves the room.

At this point, Brian says, "Some people go through the process of grief faster than others."

As audience members, we get a good laugh from this. And yet, it's true. Some people go through it faster than others.

I remember going to the funeral of a friend of mine. He was an accountant, but he had also been in the Coast Guard. I walked over to the casket and saw him lying there in his Coast Guard uniform, and I began crying.

I went outside and took a moment to connect with the GOD of my understanding. Then I went back in and looked at him again, and although there were still tears running down my cheeks, I was smiling.

Complaining is easy, and people often do it to excess. Gratitude is more difficult, but it's more useful. Even in moments of loss, and grief, and pain.

When my mind is working for me, I'm building something from it that's positive. When it's working against me, I'm tearing down what I've built. So either my mind from the old development, with all of its societal insanity takes me, or I manage it.

You've heard of the Christians who were thrown to the lions in ancient Rome, right? People were running in sheer panic, chased by lions, and others who got on their knees to pray. Some died peacefully, and some died in complete terror. Some looked to GOD, and some looked to the lion. But all had that choice.

I have choices, and rather than allowing my mind to choose for me, I choose for myself. That has been my method, even to this day. Refining myself through a process of elimination. It isn't always immediate, but it always begins with a choice. And when I make a choice, I reach to the power of GOD to effect the change.

How often have I failed to recognize when I needed to make a choice?

Too often.

I see so many people who are terrorized daily by the mind of society. It's the irrational mind, the mind that dredges up fears, and fears of fears, and fears that don't even exist. And the result of these fears is insecurity.

And who hasn't been there? Whether I'm a millionaire or the poorest man on earth, I'm subject to fears. Money makes no distinction with that.

When I first entered development, I learned that there were different acronyms for certain phrases. The first acronym for F.E.A.R. was, *Future Events Appear Real*.

F	E	A	R
u	v	p	e
t	e	p	a
u	n	e	l
r	t	a	
e	s	r	

It's not that they are real, or will be real, just that they appear real.

Now, if that future event manifested, so did the second acronym: *Frick Everything And Run*.

F	E	A	R
r	v	n	u
i	e	d	n
c	r		
k	y		
	t		
	h		
	i		
	n		
	g		

This is the one I used to practice the most.

But there is a third, and it's the only way to overcome fear.

That acronym is, **Face Everything And Recover**.

F	E	A	R
a	v	n	e
c	e	d	c
e	r		o
	y		v
	t		e
	h		r
	i		
	n		
	g		

How do we want to live? Do we want to look to GOD or look to the lions?

If I don't know how I want to live, who do I call upon to learn how?

When we were in school, there were teachers. Some taught reading, some writing, some arithmetic. A different teacher for each subject. Why is it then, that once we are out of school, we believe we no longer need guidance?

The answer: Insecurity

Insecure people don't want correction from others, because they live with constant criticism from themselves, in their own minds. In fact, they have been beating themselves up for so long that they can't stand to have someone else do it, too.

If I were about to embark on a journey across the jungle, what's the first thing I would need? A plan? A map?

How about a guide? Someone who's been there before, preferably a number of times. Someone who can lead me safely through the jungle.

Even if I were to attain enlightenment on my own, without a mentor, I would still not be a hundred percent secure because it's mine and mine alone. Anything that is mine alone is subject to change through my feelings. That is why I rely on a power greater than myself because He doesn't change. GOD is always secure, and I rely on His strength and steadfastness.

That being said, I still run my so-called messages from GOD by my spiritual advisor. I don't want to be as ignorant and foolish as those people throughout history and the world who have relied on their individual communications with GOD.

Whenever I saw what an idiot I had been, or how foolish of a thing I had just finished doing, I laughed. Why? It was because of the realization that I didn't have to do it again. When most people see that about themselves they go from feeling bad to feeling worse.

I took it as a relief. I was able to recognize my mistake, and that meant I didn't have to repeat it.

My One Bad Day

In December of 2011, I went to see my doctor. I had been experiencing a shortness of breath and decided that I should get it checked out. After a stress test and a physical, the doctor informed me that I would need surgery; a quadruple bypass.

This was on a Monday or Tuesday. The doctor asked when I wanted to have the surgery, so I said, "You're the doctor. Tell me when it should be done."

He decided I should have it done as soon as possible, and scheduled it for that Thursday.

I had my surgery on December 15th, 2011, and for me, going into surgery was as easy and carefree as having a cup of coffee. I wasn't afraid.

But when I came out of surgery, I began to experience complications. I had abstained from any drug or alcohol use for 25 years, and most of the time I didn't even take so much as a Tylenol. They had given me the proper dose of medication for a man of my size, without considering that I had no tolerance whatsoever.

What they had given me was too much, and it sent me for a loop.

I tried to communicate to them what I was experiencing, and although they were agreeing with me, they weren't connecting the dots. For the first time in 25 years, I was out of control physically.

My doctor wasn't there at that time, so the person in charge of the hospital came to talk to me, but I soon came to the conclusion that he was like Dr. House. He didn't seem to care about my situation or condition.

After he went away, I began to believe I was being left to die. That was not reality, but at that moment, it was my reality.

Even in that state, I knew I needed to reach out for help. At that time, I was a spiritual advisor to a man who happened to be a doctor. I called him up, and after talking with him I knew what I needed to do; I needed to separate my mind from my body, so the body would no longer have an effect on my emotions.

After reaching out to my friend and the GOD of my understanding, I found peace. I believed it was my time, and that I was going to die, but there was no fear. I waited to stop breathing, but I did not worry.

I used to believe it was difficult to let go. One day when I was angry, I looked up at the sky (which was the way I connected with GOD at that time), and asked why it's so hard to let go. The response that came to me was that it is actually more difficult to hold on when what I'm holding is anger, pain or difficulties.

My wife, Neva, wasn't in the room at that moment, but my sister, Nora, was. I began to tell Nora what needed to be done when I was gone.

When I say that in the last 32 years I have had only one bad day, this was it. And not because I thought I might die. It was because of the realization that the drugs were in charge of my body at that moment. It was like being unconscious for the first time in 25 years.

A conscious person will not accept a state of unconsciousness. I had been conscious for a long time and had worked diligently at managing my mind, and my thoughts. As a result of the surgery, the staff had tried to send me into a state of unconsciousness.

Sometimes I will see a person going through development, but not really being in it. And eventually, when they aren't in it, they leave. But the only people who choose to abandon their development are those who have never truly achieved *real consciousness.* Likewise, the only people who decide to go back into unconsciousness are those who were *never really conscious to begin with.*

Losing consciousness was not something I wanted, because there is no life in unconsciousness, and I had been conscious for a long time.

My trust may not show with all things, but it shows with the big things. But the thing about trust is that it doesn't exist until it's being demonstrated. Until that moment, it's just a notion of what may be.

When I was in real estate, I went to look at a house. The woman there had many religious artifacts and icons throughout the home, and as I looked through the interior, she told me about her faith and how marvelous it was.

But when I asked her to step outside with me so we could inspect the exterior, she hesitated.

It was cloudy outside, she explained. She might get struck by lightning.

Her faith dropped from a 10 to a 2.

I tried my first cigarette when I was thirteen or fourteen and was a smoker until 2008. I smoked a pack and a half (sometimes two) a day, but I'll tell you how I quit.

GOD, I turn my smoking over to the care of you, and it's easy.

And that made it easier for me to give up smoking.

The first week or two I was confronted with a number of thoughts and temptations, but I kept on practicing in faith. I observed that during certain situations and at certain times I would get cravings. For example, when I would have a sip of coke, after eating, after sex, and every time I had nothing to do.

This lasted for a few days, but they were not overwhelming. I began to recognize these calling cards. When I saw them as a force of habit, I stopped giving those thoughts value because they I could see they had no value.

After two weeks I didn't have a problem any longer, or any obsessive thoughts about it. I also recognized that smoking had become a habit and that so often when I smoked, it was a result of an automatic subconscious reaction to whatever else I happened to be doing at the time.

I haven't had the desire to smoke since then, and seldom a thought about it.

Cigarettes were just one more thing that was controlling me, but through trust in GOD, and turning that over to the care of GOD, I haven't smoked not one puff since, and that was January 31st of 2008.

Faith and Freedom

When I first thought of writing this book, two words came to mind. One is *faith*. The other is *freedom*.

Throughout the ages, it has been said that the eyes are the windows of the spirit. Early in my development I became intrigued with this concept and started telling people about it. So one day, I was in my apartment when I said to myself, *Richard, you've been telling people about the eyes being the windows of the spirit. How about yours?*

I went to the bathroom mirror and looked into my own eyes, but I didn't see the freedom or happiness I had been talking about.

I began to look at why my eyes were displaying sadness. I considered my life and my situation at that time and realized I was unhappy with the relationship I was in.

I had found myself hooked up with a woman who, for lack of a better word, was nuts. One moment she was satisfied, the next she was unhappy. One minute things were fine, the next they weren't. She was making me crazy and toying with my emotions all the time.

So I let her go, and when I looked again at my eyes, I noticed the improvement.

Freedom is a marvelous feeling.

But to have freedom, I must first have faith, and the reason that I had no faith for so much of my life (that is to say, I had no trust) was because trust was removed from me at such an early age. Not only through those two rapes, but also by the society which surrounded me, as well as my parents.

My mother was as good a woman as she knew how to be, but there was a lot of room for development. At best, she had graduated from primary school, and although she read a lot, this did more to promote her ego than her development or intelligence.

My father, on the other hand, was quite sophisticated in many ways. In his role as an orthodontic surgeon, he served the elite of Buenos Aires. He had an appreciation for music and enjoyed the works of Tchaikovsky, Beethoven, and Mozart. He was a reasonably accomplished musician himself and played at least a half-dozen instruments. But despite his studies and accomplishments, he was not any less ignorant than my mother.

Actually, in light of his education and accomplishments, one could say he was even more ignorant.

Whether I am a simple graduate of primary school or a scholar with several Ph.D.s, the only thing that really matters is what I'm doing about life. Am I a happy person, or an unhappy person?

If I have a Ph.D., and I am well respected in my field, perhaps wealthy as well, and yet I'm unhappy, I am no better off than the person who only finished primary school.

In 1986, I had many accomplishments. The stores, the houses, the cars, the family, the girlfriends. *Yet I had nothing because I had lost myself.*

When I began to develop, I first had to believe there could be something better. As I studied, and learned, and grew, I was then able to build trust.

One of the definitions of faith is blind trust, but in reality, the word blind is unnecessary, because there is either trust or there isn't. I can't try to develop trust. I either trust, or I do not. To have faith is to have trust.

I have trust. The many miraculous things in my life and the many things I have been able to do and come through unscathed have proven to me that my trust, a majority of the time, is there.

Both in life, and near death, because I have had those experiences as well.

There can only be freedom for me when there is trust. If I have freedom based on my own understanding, it will last only to the moment that feelings change regarding that understanding.

It may be possible for some people to have freedom without faith, but there will be an imbalance there, and in a moment of insecurity, they will not have anyone to trust.

When that happens, there will be no one there for them to rely on.

(How is it that I wake up at midnight, and I'm worrying about money when I'm making more than 99% of the people in the world? What am I going to be doing at midnight about this anyway? I should be going to sleep, not worrying about this nonsense.)

Chapter 7

Mentors

One of the things I came to see was that all of my beliefs were developed through my own intelligence or lack thereof. The trick to overcoming this was to come out of myself and expose these beliefs to the intelligence of others. Not just my secrets, even the things I consider good and true.

I know a man who calls me *spiritual advisor*. He's actually been working on his development longer than I, but one big difference between the two of us is that although he goes to gatherings with other people in development, he doesn't invest much (if any) time in studying. On the other hand, I've studied many sources that have complemented my growth and furthered my understanding.

More important, I have had mentors. He has never had a true partner in his development. He's been doing it all on his own. To truly develop an understanding one needs to do more than just be a part of the gathering – one needs to participate.

And one needs a mentor.

When I align myself with someone else, I unlock a wealth of development and understanding. In the very beginning, I found a mentor who had only been developing himself for a year or two. After some time, I began to see the gaps in his knowledge and understanding, but there was one thing he did for me that has benefited me ever since.

He made a student out of me.

I had never been a student. Even when I was in school, I was never a student. When I went to school, I generally missed 40 or 50 days a year, and I had to finish it at night. Plus, after my father left, my primary objective was survival and contributing to the family, so being a student was never much of a priority.

This first mentor encouraged my growth and made suggestions. By following these suggestions, I began to surpass his understanding in less than a year.

After that, I found someone who had been in development for five years. I don't know if I surpassed his understanding or not, but generally speaking, concerning my level of serenity, tranquility, and happiness, my life has been a better one than any I've been exposed to.

The key to growth and evolvement, I began to understand, is that my mind needed to be expanded, but not by me. Rather than trying to expand my own mind, I needed to allow my mind to be expanded by others.

There's a quote by Herbert Spencer which goes, ***"There is a principle which is a bar against all information, which is proof against all arguments, and which cannot fail to keep a man in everlasting ignorance – that principle is contempt prior to investigation."***

Before taking the communication course previously mentioned, I approached every conversation with contempt prior to investigation. Anytime I spoke with someone, I was trying to establish what it was they were saying, how I would reply, and why they didn't know what they were talking about anyhow.

I never listened. And that was one reason why I never developed much of an understanding.

The key, I learned, is to hear only what is being said, rather than my own internal talk.

The English poet John Donne wrote, years ago, that no man is an island. Yet when I look back on my life, and the lives of others, that is all so many of us have ever been. Islands of insecurity and irrational fears. Islands of doubt and frustration. Islands shaped and eroded by the mind of society.

But it doesn't have to be that way, and the more I've exposed myself to others, the more whole I've become.

There are a lot of people who will talk the game, but the game is not the mind, the game is being. The mind is an essential tool, and it's crucial for us to learn how to use it, but the goal is not the tool, the goal is living a happy life. When looking for a mentor, this is important to understand.

Say I'm in a room with 30 other people, and I can see all of their expressions and eyes. I might see one that is alright, who has a pleasant personality. He is okay with life. I might see another who is somewhat tranquil; he doesn't have a pleasant or unpleasant personality. Two or three like this are the most I will find out of the 30.

The others have a look like*, Life really sucks. When is it going to get better?*

They might say that life is better than it was before and that they are really happy, but if I went from being horrible to being merely bad to others, then that is still no great improvement, in reality.

When I'm looking for a mentor, I look for someone who speaks positively and has a positive expression. Someone who speaks honestly and with love, for **love without honesty is hypocrisy, and honesty without love is cruelty**. A good mentor will find a balance between the two.

Without daily mentorship, especially in the beginning, there can be no accomplishment. It is that critical!

But no one is a perfect student. As much as I have strived to follow, at various times (being that I was a creation of John Wayne), I have debated the mentorship. But one of the things I'm thankful for is that, by the grace of GOD, my debates have been short ones. I have observed people who argue to their own death, and even though they were breathing, nevertheless they were dead. From what I have seen, many people are breathing, but they aren't living.

141

Mentorship has been important for me and continues to be important. I wouldn't study a manual for an F-35, and then go to the Airforce and ask to fly one without any guidance or training. Yet, we often do just that with our lives. We make critical decisions without any input, and then wonder why things end up in a mess.

As many wise people have known throughout the ages, it is beneficial for even the most spiritual person to have their understanding and what they believe to be guidance from GOD checked by another spiritual person.

When I arrive at some magnificent idea or communication from GOD, I get with someone who I know is equally developed, or ahead of me, and see what they think of it. In the beginning, most of my ideas weren't even worth discussing. These days, most of the time, they are good ideas.

When I speak to my mentor at this stage in my development, we typically talk about how good life is and how we enjoy it.

The lawyer who defends himself has a fool for a client, and development is the same way. Why would I want to deny myself the benefit of having another intelligence helping me progress?

Not only is it egotistical, but it's also extremely stupid.

When two minds develop together (with one ahead of the other, preferably), there is a better chance for faster growth. There is a difference between wisdom and intelligence, and the difference is this; ***intelligence is when I learn from my mistakes, wisdom is when I learn from the mistakes of others.***

The things I've learned from my own intelligence have cost me much more, emotionally as well as financially, than they would have had I practiced more wisdom.

As good as I have become in certain respects, there is still a great deal of improvement I can make. When I saw that I was the most ignorant human being in the world, I saw this through just a tiny crack of understanding.

I'm still the most ignorant human being in the world (concerning my own development), but ***now I'm looking through wide-open doors.***

The key to the development that I have experienced to this point is that it was not achieved by myself. I have people that were ahead in life guiding me through the different stages. Every time I surpassed one, I went and looked for another one that was still ahead of me.

Even today, I still have a person that I utilize as a guide. I don't know whether he is ahead of me, but I do know that we communicate on a level that we can both enjoy.

Most of the time when I call him about something minor, it's to communicate what I'm going to do about it. He either agrees with my decision or asks 'really?' and I know what he means. I don't live the life of a genius. The things that occur in my life are to a large degree simple. Simple problems require simple solutions, and he has an abundance of those.

Put simply, there is nothing more important for me than to continue to reach out to people who are ahead of me during my development. The only thing I have had to give up when I was seeking mentorship was the misery that I used to call a life.

Today, I live an enriched one.

The Problem

Most people who want to make a personal change have no problem jumping in. In the beginning, they are excited and enthused. The problem, as I have observed, is that they don't get far enough to begin receiving the reward. They only want to get to a certain point, so they can then coast. But **coasting is only downhill. You can't coast uphill.** (I haven't practiced coasting to any great degree, but on certain things I have. I have coasted in regard to this book for 20, perhaps 25 years – and yet, it is so much more now than it would have been then!)

They give up too quickly, and subsequently, are left with just the work of it.

Most people believe they have already worked enough, on everything, and it's time for them to get what is due.

I never went to school to read or write English. I never went to school to speak it. If you were to hear me speak, you would hear that I have a heavy accent. I couldn't teach myself to pronounce the words because the only time I knew how I sounded saying them was when I listened to myself on a recording.

However, if you were to spend much time with me, you would find that my English vocabulary is quite profuse.

I taught myself. And the reason I was so successful at teaching myself was that I got deep enough into the learning that *it became a pleasure* instead of a job. Most people don't get that far. And some of the few that do get close enough stop there, because that's only as far as they wanted to get, and for them, that's good enough.

The goal for me is to become involved enough in my studies so that I receive the pleasure of it.

(If my English is not better than it is, it is because I was the teacher!)

As mentioned, the first mentor I found had only been in development a year or two. When I was about six months into my development, I began to see that he lacked certain things, so I began to ask other people about it.

But the thing I did not do was quit in the middle. There was a specific process which needed to be followed, and until this process had ended, I didn't get another teacher. Some students become too intelligent too quickly and dump their mentor, but they do so to their own detriment. Despite his deficits, I stayed with my mentor until the time was right to find another.

But this first mentor, Bernie, made a student out of me, and to this day, over 32 years since first becoming a student, *I am still a student.*

The only difference between then and now is the vast majority of the time I can tell when I need to lead as well as when I need to follow. I'm comfortable in either position. I can also tell when a person is ahead of me, and when they are behind me.

When I see them doing the same ignorant actions I used to do, I know that they're behind me.

I am careful, however, not to drift into condemnation. The problem I used to have with judging is that it always carried condemnation. It wasn't that people were stupid in my assessment, it was that in my condemnation, there were going to remain stupid forever. And how could I know something like that?

Taking on a mentor was unusual for me. I was never the type of person to ask for direction from anyone. One of the main components of being shy and lacking confidence is the need to be one's own director.

I had done that for far too long.

Correcting Without Concern

When I first started this journey, there was a greater need for studying, and instruction, and mentorship. But as I've evolved, so have my needs. Today, my journey is more about smoothing out the rough areas of my life, whatever they may be.

And though I make an effort to smooth those rough areas, I'm not concerned with them. The reason I'm not concerned is because I'm not GOD. Anytime I'm worried about something, anytime I declare that life isn't going right, I'm playing GOD. When I'm playing GOD, what I'm actually saying is, *GOD, you need to get your act together. You're not doing it right.*

I have faith, and faith is trust. I can trust GOD because He is a GOD of love. How could I claim to be a person of faith and not trust GOD? Furthermore, if I trust GOD, how can I live my life in fear and trepidation?

In the beginning, when I would call my advisor and share my thoughts or ideas, I was almost always wrong. Today, most of the time, he agrees with me.

How long did that take to accomplish?

I can't really pinpoint the moment my life became easy, but from the very beginning, it became easier. My life certainly became easier when I stopped blaming everyone else because then I became responsible for my own life. I had no more excuses. There's only one reason for everything to be someone else's fault.

It's so I don't have to do anything about it.

It's always easier to place the blame on someone else because then it's them who needs to get their stuff together, not me. And if we recall, the displacement of personal responsibility is a character disorder.

But when I establish that whatever is happening is not the cause of my problems, but rather how I am reacting to whatever is happening, I am able to see a new level of reality. Once I accept that, then I have something I can do about my internal strife. What I can do is take responsibility for my own reaction.

We usually only want to get well up to our point of comfort. Not real, lasting comfort, of course, but comfort in the present moment. That's why we hear so many people describe their life as a rollercoaster. Up and down, up and down.

I used to say, I'll be alright when this happens. I'll be alright when these people do what I want them to do.

Today I'm alright, and those people are still not doing what I want them to do.

I don't guide too many people, because not too many are willing to get involved enough so that the work becomes a pleasure. And getting someone to follow the protocols can be difficult. Often, they will call and report only after they've done something. When they do, I tell them I don't need a reporter.

To evolve as a student of life, I must follow first. If I'm still learning about how to live life, then I should call my advisor and get my idea checked before I do something. That way, I can change course if necessary. It's more energy to mess up and to clean up that mess than to do it right from the start.

For the people who utilize me as an advisor, I share with them, and suggest to them what to study, and ask them to call me every day to speak about it. It's that simple. And what could be better?

But it takes work. It takes effort. It takes a guide who knows the way.

And it takes the willingness to follow.

Generalities Versus Specifics

One of the things I first had to learn was to look for similarities, not differences, and not generalities. I have never progressed by working with generalizations. It takes specifics.

In a general way, before I began to develop my understanding, I was screwed up. Part of the reason I stayed that way was because I never pinpointed why I was screwed up.

After my mother came to the states, I was left to live with my grandmother, but she was seldom there. The uncle that lived with us at that time was only present at night to sleep. Quite often my oldest sister received the money my mother sent and procured it for herself.

At one point, there was no food and no money. But rather than ask for help, I simply did without.

My father's three brothers lived just a few blocks away. I could have gone there to eat at any time. My father's sister lived seven blocks away. I could have gone there, as well.

I'm sure I could have gone to one of my friends' houses, but I didn't want to do that, either.

To me, asking for help meant defeat. It was an admission to my own personal powerlessness and weakness, and I would not demonstrate that under any circumstances. For six days I went without eating, and I probably would have died of hunger rather than ask for help. That's how secretive I was.

In the first six months of my development, I spoke more than I did during the first 37 years of my life.

When I maintain something in the shadows, obscured and generalized, there is no way to overcome it. I must be specific.

Take shyness for instance. For so long I had held onto that title. I was shy, and since I kept reaffirming to myself that I was shy, I kept acting as if I were shy.

When I began to overcome shyness, I first had to identify it as a specific problem. Then I had to stop labeling myself with that title and affirming something I didn't want to be.

During this process, I had to look back on my life and uncover when this shyness first began to manifest. What were the proofs to that shyness?

Was it because my mother and father separated, and I felt I was a poor little boy who didn't have enough? Was it that I was raped by my uncle? Or the teenager with the bicycle?

I had to go back to determine the source, and one thing that was most harming to me, indeed, was the two times I was raped. I had kept those incidents obscured and generalized. I never wanted to confront them and certainly never wanted to share them with anyone.

It wasn't until I listened to others, and saw how maintaining secrets had been the root of their troubles, that I understood what I needed to do.

I needed to be specific in confronting what had plagued me.

And anytime I want to make any change in my life, be it small or large, I must be absolutely specific about what that problem is, and what I need to do to correct it.

Every day we hear politicians speaking in generalities. They give us titles, but no context. They give us outlines, but no facts. When we do hear the facts, they are so brief that we have to catch them amongst the thousands of generalities we've been given.

If I'm serious about my growth and development, then there are only four answers I should utilize. These answers are direct, and they are specific. They are as follows:

- Yes
- No
- I know
- I don't know

General answers are a detriment to my development. Examples of these are:

- I think so
- Possibly
- Maybe
- Who knows?
- Uh-huh

And any number of other non-specific responses.

When I say "Yes" or "No," I'm assuming responsibility for myself. When I say "Maybe" or "Possibly," I can't be held accountable for whatever occurs.

The problem isn't just that others can't hold me accountable, it's that I don't have to hold myself accountable. If I don't hold myself accountable, and take personal responsibility, then I can't change.

If I went to the bank and asked for a loan, and the banker told me, "Maybe," what am I going to think? If I then go home and tell my wife that the banker said, "Maybe," what's she supposed to think? Will she feel very secure about the loan?

Most people don't want to be decisive, because then they'll be accountable for their decisions.

In Scott Peck's book *The Road Less Traveled*, he speaks about discipline and explains that people with a character disorder almost never get well because they never assume responsibility for anything. It's always other people's fault, or society's fault, his fault, her fault, your fault. . .

But never my fault.

Of course, neurotics do the opposite. They assume everything is their fault. And though they have their responsibilities misplaced, they are at least assuming responsibility. They just need to learn to assign it properly and bring it to balance.

I believe there is a GOD, and the GOD I have is constant. He doesn't say maybe, or possibly. When I pray, He doesn't shrug his shoulders. He doesn't say who knows? We'll see.

He is decisive and specific.

Glossary

Below is a list of words that have been important to me. These definitions are accurate in terms of my experience and development, and that is what makes them the truth for me.

Acceptance: Peace developed through understanding.

Altruism: For the wellbeing of others.

Character Disorder: Inability to assume responsibility.

Confidence: With trust.

Confront: To face up to.

Discipline: Comes from the word disciple, meaning follower of GOD.

Discover: To search and study.

Drunk: 1) Inebriated or under the influence of a mood / mind altering substance. 2) Overwhelmed by emotions.

Faith: Blind trust.

Grace: A free gift.

Happiness: A heavenly state.

Heaven: Happiness.

Humility: The ability to see things as they are (not as I would like them to be).

Insanity: An inability to see reality in a way that benefits me.

Knowledge: The ability to practice something, as opposed to just having information.

Love: Anything done that is positive to anything or anyone, including myself.

Meditate: To think about.

Misthinking: Any thought not used for constructing. To think is to build upon.

Neurotic: Assuming responsibility for what isn't mine.

Obsession: A reality that lies beneath the conscious level.

Prayer: Any serious thought, whether positive or negative.

Sober: While sober can have multiple definitions, just about all of them pertain to balance.

Spiritual Principles: A truth that cannot be changed or adulterated by anyone or everyone, in reality. 1) As a man thinks it in his heart, so is it. 2) What you sow, you reap.

Spirituality: 1) Gives life to the physical. 2) is the highest form of reality there is.

Textbook: A book with principles to study and practice. A textbook is not a reading book.

Trying: Not doing.

Understanding: From the Greek language, to stand safely under the tree.

Will: An action in the past tense.

Willingness: Doing something at the *earliest possible* moment. (neither when I wish to do it, nor when I think I should do it)

Wisdom: Learning from the mistakes of others. Intelligence is learning from my own mistakes.

(How is it that I wake up late at night and I start thinking about work or worrying about yesterday or having a conversation with myself about tomorrow, and I can't even do anything at that hour in the night? Who sent me those thoughts? I definitely didn't call for them.)

Chapter 8

Happy When?

I will be happy. . .

When?

That's how I used to live. I will be happy when I get this girl. I will be happy when I get that car. I will be happy when I make more money.

Unfortunately, when I finally got those things, I still wasn't happy.

I didn't become happy until I learned to deal with me. I had to learn to manage my mind. Though I'm still not capable of completely managing it, I am able to manage it most of the time. Even when my mind tells me something crazy, or negative, it seldom disturbs me. Why? Because I know what to do.

What I usually do first is call the person I trust most and run it by him. Most of the time he tells me it's okay. Once in a while, he says to me, "Really?" and I know what that means.

When I used to get depressed, it was often the result of an unfulfilled want. I couldn't do this, or I couldn't have that. It was typically about the baby not getting what he wanted.

I came to see that depression is a title, just like shyness, or anxiety, or any number of ways of being. It's a title given to a set of behaviors, and those behaviors were shaped by the way I used to think and live. There is no depression. What kept me depressed were my unfulfilled desires and wants, whether it was the girl, the car, the money, the job, or my happiness.

I was the most oblivious when I was a rich man. I had become a human doer. And even though I was doing things that were supposedly fun, I experienced nothing, because what you find in oblivion is nothing. Having a wife and two girlfriends? That's supposed to be fun. Going on trips and weekend getaways and zipping around in a Porsche? That's supposed to be fun.

But I was lost.

Many people are just like I used to be. Lost in oblivion, unhappy with their situation, and suffering. Unfortunately, there are more who die in oblivion than come out of it. Do you know anyone like that?

Many people complain about their job, and yet they stay. Why? Is it the boss's fault? Is it because we can't risk changing? Or can't make as much money somewhere else?

Or is it our choice?

We stay because of our fears and insecurities. I often stayed in bad relationships, bad jobs, and bad situations because I didn't see that I had a choice. I could choose how I wanted to live my life, and *I could choose happiness.*

Whenever I am unhappy, I am harboring negative feelings. When I harbor negative feelings about a person or a situation, I am playing GOD. When I am playing GOD, I am declaring that my judgment is greater than His.

I haven't forgiven anyone, but that's because I haven't had to. *Forgiveness is GOD's job, and He has already done it*. My job is to align myself with GOD's forgiveness because He is steadfast and unchanging. The teenager who raped me, the father that left us hanging in the air, the uncle that abused me, the bullies that tormented me, and the girls who ripped me off; GOD has forgiven me, and all of them, as well. So I have no right to carry ill feelings towards anyone.

Including myself. I am not guilty of any nor all the lousy things I've done. I'm responsible for each and every one of them, but I'm not guilty. I have made amends for all the ones I could, and the ones I was allowed to. And GOD has forgiven me for all of the ones I have harmed, just as **He has forgiven all the ones who harmed me**.

The best I can do for myself and anyone else is to demonstrate a pleasant life, at the least. One that is not encumbered by seriousness, or sadness, or disturbances. And I've never seen a happy person that doesn't smile.

GOD is Waiting

As much as I've progressed, I know there is still ignorance within me that I need to expel. But I've arrived at the most wonderful state there is: I've come to the conclusion that I'm not GOD. So from the moment I establish that

I'm not GOD, and ***I believe in a GOD of love, I can no longer beat up on myself.***

Anytime I beat up on myself, I'm practicing unforgiveness toward myself. I'm playing GOD and exercising GOD's power. How often do we exercise GOD's power against ourselves, and then turn around and ask, "GOD, why are you doing this to me?"

Remember when I shared how I learned to smile? I prayed and prayed for GOD to teach me how to smile, and I did that for a year and a half without ever smiling. I finally realized that all I had to do was begin to smile, and to state, "Thank you, GOD, for having taught me how to smile."

It wasn't GOD that was holding me back. It was me.

Most people live in a constant state of waiting. Waiting to feel well, waiting to be whole, waiting for life to get better, and they get angry because GOD isn't doing what they want. But so often while we are waiting on GOD, GOD is waiting on us.

Prior to developing an understanding of GOD, I believed in luck. Anything that happened that most people would consider miraculous to some degree, I attributed to chance, randomness, and being in the right place at the right time. But when I began to learn about reality, and see the truth of how my life had been, as well as my shortcomings and ignorance, I began to see how many times GOD had intervened on my behalf.

When I began to see the ignorance of my life, the stupidity of my life, the grief of my life, I wanted to get better. When I realized I had been the most ignorant human being I had known, I began to dedicate hours of each day towards study and development. I didn't do that for a few days, or a couple of weeks, or a month or two. I did it for years. How much have you dedicated to your development? *If development were a job, would you hire yourself?*

Through all of that study and meditation, I developed trust. I realized that I have a GOD who can do all things, and He can do them without me worrying about it. I don't want to have the small god I had before. I've learned that when I don't feel good about something, it's for two reasons: I am playing GOD, and I'm not practicing what I've learned.

I value the life GOD has given me, and I'm not willing to trade it for stupidity. When I die, those problems aren't going with me. Nor is my car, nor my house, nor my wife, nor my son, nor the weather.

So why worry about them?

I once heard a person say, "I just don't scratch things that don't itch."

I used to practice the opposite all the time. I would worry myself over nothing, and create problems that didn't exist. I could do this for hours, days, or even longer. Why? To what purpose?

After all, I still have four fingers by the grace of GOD.

When I was 10 or 12 years old, I would occasionally go with an uncle of mine, a brother of my father, to help lay tiles. The uncle had a son, my cousin, who suffered from multiple sclerosis.

One day we were traveling to a job site in an old-fashioned enclosed van as one might see in the 1940s or 50s. The driver was on the right side, and so I was seated on the left, which would normally be the driver's side.

My uncle was driving quite rapidly through the streets, and I started to become fearful in response to his recklessness.

As we passed a corner, something came to me, a vision of sorts.

When we get to the next corner, we're going to get hit from his side. It's going to send the van this way. My door is going to open up. I'm going to be thrown outside. I'm going to land against the curb.

And the tire is going to smash my head.

We got to the corner. We got hit on his side. My door came open. I was thrown out. I landed with my head next to the curb. I opened my eyes.

And the tire stopped an inch from my face.

I don't know what all of that means, whether it was a premonition or something else, but I do know it was miraculous.

Out of my own stupidity, I've almost drowned twice. I'm one of the few people in this world that suffered a burst appendix while learning to scuba dive without knowing how to swim.

I had gone to the Bahamas with a woman I was seeing, and we went into a pool that was 20 or 30 feet deep to prepare for the actual dive the following day. It was a good thing because had this happened in the ocean, I would have probably died.

That night my appendix ruptured, and I ended up in the hospital. While there, the intravenous needle slipped from my arm and fell to a floor that many years before had been white. The nurse picked it up, wiped it off, and stuck it back in my arm. And that was the nicest part of that experience.

Today, I have a relationship with GOD. That means I can relate to GOD. If I'm not relating to GOD, then I have a relation, not a relationship. The main characteristic is that I trust Him. If I have a relationship, that means I am in communication with the GOD of my understanding. If I have a relation, then I just trust without communicating.

We often confuse religion with a relationship, but often times the people who have religion don't have a relationship. They live in the same fear and trepidation as everyone else. Anyone who has a relationship with GOD will live in freedom, not fear. This is why, when I speak of GOD, I don't speak of Him in terms of any one religion, but rather regarding my relationship with Him; what I know, what I believe, how it has operated, and how it continues to operate.

If one were to ask me if I expect to go to Heaven, my answer is this; "I'm still dealing with earth. I'll let you know when I get there."

Getting myself to Heaven is not my job, anyhow. *I have a GOD of unconditional love, and He is a forgiving GOD.* All I need to do is go along with the love and forgiveness He has already provided. *What kind of GOD do you have?*

One of my spiritual advisors says that the best one can be is 'good for nothing.' That means that one isn't even good for the purpose of going to Heaven. One is just good for the sake of being good. Anything worth doing is an end in itself. On the other hand, **anything done to an end is self-robbery.**

The definition of happiness is *a heavenly state.* To me, that is my relationship with GOD and all of the things GOD has already provided when He laid the foundation of the universe.

All of the many blessings and miracles He is waiting for us to accept and receive and enjoy.

Unconditional Love

In my understanding (or misunderstanding), unconditional love exists when I'm willing to share with you or show you the truth, even if it means you dislike me.

So **unconditional love is when I care enough about you that I don't care about me**.

Now, it doesn't mean that you can do whatever you want and that I should stand for it. Unconditional love also doesn't mean unconditional giving. If I give you something that is negative or has a derogatory effect on your life, that is not love.

Unconditional love is when I care enough about you that I don't care how you'll react towards me. After all, love without honesty is hypocrisy, and honesty without love is cruelty. If I love someone, I will be honest with them, even if they become reactive as a result. This doesn't mean, however, that I have to become a pushover. I don't allow the love GOD has instilled within me to be abused by others. That would be a disservice to GOD, and **love is anything that is positive toward anyone or anything, including me.**

Take a dysfunctional relationship, for instance. If I remain in a dysfunctional relationship in an effort to practice unconditional love, the relationship will never improve. My attachment to that situation creates the feeling in the other party that they are right, and that there is no need to change their behavior. After all, I'm still with them. If they were wrong, I would have left already, right?

One of the best ways to begin practicing unconditional love is to start looking for the similarities, rather than the differences.

I once volunteered to visit prisoners at a maximum-security facility in Palestine, Texas, where I would speak to convicts. The drive was long, about a hundred miles one way, but I felt this was an important act of service, and so I began going every weekend.

I stopped going when I saw that I was there more than they were, and they lived there. My motto is, **use, but don't abuse**, and my time was being abused.

Often times in the past I have excused myself, as I've seen many people do since then, by using these four standard answers (that prevented me from developing myself):

- *"Yes, but. . ."*
- *"You don't understand."*
- *"I'm different."*
- *"Ya, I know that."*

But if I know so much already, why am I so unhappy?

There are so many ways we can give these four answers, without actually saying them. I can tell a person they don't understand, by saying, "Well, I'm in retail, and you're in manufacturing, so you can't see it the same way." Or, "I'm in sales, and you drive a truck. . . world of difference."

But no matter how I phrase it, it always comes down to one of those four answers, and when I give one of those four answers, I'm focusing on the differences rather than the similarities.

On occasion, of course, there will be a genuine misunderstanding. The way I sort that out is I continue to press on the subject whenever the opportunity arises. I do so diplomatically, of course, and I look for the similarities, and I practice unconditional love. However, I also am aware that there may come a time when I need to gather my marbles and leave the game.

One of the things I learned in this new way of life is that after a while I began to see myself in every man, woman, and child. That is part of unconditional love, as well. It's about having empathy and being empathetic.

Even though I have never been a child molester or murderer like some of the men in that prison, even though I have never become an alcoholic who drinks every day, and even though I never became addicted to drugs, as a result of the sex addiction I used to have, I can see myself in every one of those people. I look for the similarities rather than the differences, and addiction is addiction regardless of what shape it takes.

On the surface, we may all appear different, but all of the differences are the things we've learned from our parents, our friends, our neighbors, our teachers. . . in other words, these differences are what we've picked up from the mind of society: our inhibitions or lack of inhibitions; our shame or our shamelessness; our wants and desires; and our fears.

Beneath this inherited mind of society is a human being, and we are more similar than different.

If I'm playing poker, and another man is playing the ponies, and another is putting money into a risky investment, we are all three gambling. If you're a workaholic, and I'm an alcoholic, we are both reaching for distractions.

What that distraction happens to be isn't as important as the outcome, and the outcome often points to one thing and one thing only; the mind of society.

So, what is the common denominator?

Insanity.

And what is insanity?

An inability to see reality in a way that benefits me.

Whether I was a poor boy in Argentina who had not eaten for six or seven days, or a successful businessman speeding around in a Porsche 928, if I am unable to see reality in a way that benefits me, then I am only in survival mode.

When I was in survival mode, I was not living.

So even when I compare myself at two ages and two very different places in my life, I can see the similarities there, rather than the differences.

And when I look for the similarities between myself and other people, I am better able to understand them, and better able to be peaceful and happy. The peace comes when I see them continuing to do the same stupid or ignorant things I used to do and no longer practice the vast majority of the time. Doesn't it make you happy to no longer look stupid or ignorant?

Ignorance

Before I went to Minnesota and asked for help, I was totally detached from reality. I didn't think so, of course, but I was. I existed in three states, constantly cycling between them, and those three states were ***oblivion, anger, and rage.***

What did I find in oblivion?

Nothing. Because nothing was ever good enough. And nothing was ever bad enough, either. I didn't feel either extreme. I was ignorant to all of it, and I was emotionally dead.

Just like the phoenix, I had to burn down so I could start over again. I had to realize I needed help, admit I needed help, ask for help, and then accept the help I was given at Hazelden.

That day was the worst day of my life, and the best day, all on the same day.

When I came back from Hazelden, I went to see the parents of the girlfriend whom I had been obsessed with (and was my reason for going to Minnesota in the first place). I began telling them about the marvelous things I had experienced, but as I spoke, I could see pity developing in their eyes. I couldn't understand why they would pity me when I'd just had a life-changing experience. It wasn't until I had been in development for a year or two that it began to make sense.

What they saw in me at that time was an insane person who had just been exposed to a new level of reality, of which I had no knowledge or understanding whatsoever.

I was ignorant. . . and very excited about it!

In some areas of my life, one could argue that a certain level of ignorance has benefitted me. I've been able to achieve many difficult things, and it was because I had no limiting belief that it couldn't be done. Therefore, I had no fears or doubts.

In the 1980s, I was one of the first people I knew to link my stores via fax machine so that any one store could sell inventory from another. At the peak, we were selling over 300,000 dollars per month in dinettes. Five stores, four box trucks, a couple of vans, 40 employees, and stores in Fort Worth, Austin, Plano, Garland, Carrollton, and Dallas.

And it all started because I knew a guy in New York who had a dinette store. On my days off, I would go to his store, and we would play chess. He never explained anything about the business to me, but I noticed when he took money out of his pocket there were hundreds.

It was then that I decided I would one day open a dinette store.

So, I started my business and became successful at it, but all I really knew about were the numbers. I knew to look at the profit margin on each sale, and I knew what my overhead was for the month. I deducted one from the other, and that told me how much I had made that month.

When I later applied for a job as a management consultant, the first thing they did was send me to a seminar about business accounting. The workshop lasted five days, and by the fifth day I came to see that I really didn't know anything about running a business, and yet I had been a relatively successful business owner.

And I did it armed with only limited knowledge and the ignorance of any possible limitations.

As I believe it in my heart, so is it.

Dedication

When I decide to do something, I never look to see how long it will take or how difficult it will be. When it's finished, it's finished. I just put one foot in front of the other, and one thing at a time, also.

The key to finishing anything well is to follow someone who has already successfully walked that path. In the beginning, I had to do that until I could stop destroying myself. In other words, the best thing I did in my first year of recovery was that *I didn't listen to myself.*

I studied in the morning. I went to work. I went to a group gathering before lunch. I went to lunch with other people in development. I came back to work. After work, I went to another gathering. Then I went to dinner. After dinner, I went to yet another gathering.

Then I would go home, relax for an hour, and then study until bedtime. The following day, I did the same all over again.

In the car, I made it a point to listen to cassettes, and they weren't recordings of music.

One of my greatest sources of inspiration was a man by the name of Chuck C. I bought a set of his cassette tapes, six in all, and I've probably listened to them about 30, 40, perhaps 50 times each. And each one is over an hour long.

When I worked for the management consulting company out of Chicago, I used to visit a different city, sometimes two cities, every week. When I could, and if the next city was less than 500 miles away, I chose to drive my own car instead of flying. The reason I did this was because I could listen to cassettes all the way there and back.

By the time I got to where I was going, I was full of life from listening to all of that positivity. When I did wait at the airport, I would have an earpiece in and a portable cassette player in hand or in my pocket. I would see people getting angry over the delays and waiting times, while I was listening to Chuck C., Scott Peck, Wayne Dyer, Norman Vincent Peale, and the like. How could I get mad about waiting while listening to all of these wonderful things?

I couldn't develop positiveness while complaining. The two don't go together.

In a society where learning is supposed to be prevalent, I haven't met anybody willing to put in the same amount of time and effort toward study. I guess my mother's stubbornness finally served a good purpose.

When I choose to do something, I do it well and thoroughly. If it calls for 20, I do 21. When I first started working in America, I didn't know how to speak English. Within a few months, I had four people working under me, and they were 40 or 50 years old, while I was only 17. But whatever I did, I did with pride.

I started at a buck and a quarter per hour working for electrical contractors, and after seven months I was making $1.85. I kept asking for raises, and they kept giving them, until one day the boss said, "No. You've gotten more raises than anybody at the company!"

To which I replied, "Yes, but I'm very good."

He said he couldn't give me any more, so I gave him my two-week notice.

At my next job, I made $2.25 an hour.

I was never scared of change in my physical world. What I was afraid of was emotional change and personal change. I was scared of confronting my ignorance and dispelling it. And quite often, I was **ignorant to my ignorance.**

But to progress, to grow, and to develop, ignorance must be systematically eliminated, through study, research, and most importantly, the guidance of a good mentor.

Misthinking

After I was a couple years into this new creation of my life, I still did not understand how come I was having certain negative thoughts. Even though I had removed a great deal of my negative thinking, it seemed to me that I still had no control over what my mind sent to me. Now, I'm calling it 'my mind,' but in reality this mind was just an 'it' that had learned to dominate me. It seemed that these thoughts came to me, rather than me telling my mind what to do.

The more that I saw this negative pattern, the more that I saw I needed to do something about it. So, I began to think 'what is going on with this so-called mind of mine, that it's not working for me?' When it came to my hands and my legs, I was trained to use them. When it came to my mind, it seemed like it was trained by somebody to use me.

I thought 'how is it possible that I don't know how to manage my mind? I was sent to school and they taught me to add, multiply, and divide. But they never told me about my mind!' This mind was operating from my thoughts of inadequacy that I developed as I was growing up. These thoughts arose out of my wants and ideas of what to get in order to achieve happiness. In my own case, I could see that my ideas of what would make me happy were incorrect because I had achieved more than I ever thought I could and I was miserable. What I saw was that there was never enough, I was still miserable, and would always be miserable living that way.

Based on that realization, I was quite confused about what to do. I thought about my mind. What is a mind supposed to do? What I was beginning to realize at that time is **to think about something is to build upon. Thinking is constructive**.

Rather than me thinking all the time, I was, to a large extent, **misthinking.** On the one hand, I could think to construct whenever I was doing something for my work or my business. When it came to my personal life, however, this misthinking mind sent me all over the place. This mind was totally ridiculous.

I'll never forget the time in which I dreamt I was riding into the sunset with the most beautiful woman in the world. The next thought that came to me was 'well, what are you going to do when you see another beautiful woman? Then, you're going to be stuck with this beautiful woman!' I just had a mind that the moment it fixed me, it messed me up right afterwards. I was always in a state of transition, and I don't know what I was transitioning from. This misthinking mind was not giving me freedom. I was a slave to my misthinking.

What can be done to correct this misthinking mind?

The reason that I'm sharing this book with people is because I don't want anyone to suffer as much as I did due to my own ignorance. I can see that there are way too many people suffering unnecessarily today. We need to teach our children how to use their minds. To think rather than to misthink.

The reason we as a society have so many difficulties today is the great level of ignorance that exists within people who do hideous things, **whatever those hideous things are.** Remember, love is anything done that is positive to anything or anyone, including myself.

We need to start teaching children how to use their minds. This perspective is unique.

185

Children will need to be taught by people who don't have a clue how to manage their own minds! These children will learn the theory and then demonstrate the principles to others, so they all may develop reality.

Like I said, even though I have a great deal of advancement, by no means can I walk on water. I don't expect to walk on water. I do expect for things to get better. The more that we can teach children, and even grown-ups how to think, which is to construct, the better off we all are.

Eastern philosophy states that *'the thinking mind is a wonderful servant or a horrible master.'* When I heard that for the first time, I came to the realization that this misthinking mind that I have is actually supposed to be working for me. About the only time that this mind had ever been working for me was when I was at work or creating things for my business. I was already constructing something, so the creating mind was very beneficial for my materialistic development. At one point, I had grown to have 5 stores, 3 houses, and a brand-new Porsche 928. I was doing quite well materially, but in my personal life, I was still troubled by many different things. I was anxious about what people thought of me and even what I thought of them. I was still living a life in which I was always trying to look good for somebody else.

In those days, 99% of my conversations were inside of my head. *I never really talked to anyone and I never listened to anyone for that matter* because there was so much talk inside of my head. It is impossible for me to hear you while I am talking to me at the same time. Thank GOD that I was never in charge of an airport tower, there would have been a lot of crashes.

The question is: how is it that I can get this mind to be working for me?

First, I began to see myself and saw the amount of negativity that I was experiencing almost all the time.

Then, whenever I received a negative thought or an insane thought, I either replaced it with something positive or just sent it away. At times the way that I sent my insane thoughts away was 'really after all this time? Are you kidding me?' The most valuable practice at this time was calling the person I chose to be my guide and getting his feedback.

As time passed, I taught myself how to manage the negative thoughts that came into my mind.

Today, the vast majority of the time, even though I'm doing extremely well with my peacefulness, serenity and happiness, I still get thoughts that come out of left field. When that happens, I manage them pretty well most of the time. When I am having a bad thought or something derogative within my life, it's really not anything that is tremendous. It's just a thought that has come into my mind. Now that I've learned to manage those thoughts most of the time, my life has become good.

My life is not my happiness. My happiness is my life.

Shortcomings

When I started to look back in the beginning pages of my life, I saw that I was made little by this misthinking mind starting from when I was first raped at 5 years old. For many years afterwards, I told people that I was a real rebel. When my mother dropped me off at kindergarten school, by the time she returned home, she would find me already back inside the house. After doing that for a month or two, she got tired and said I did not have to start that year in school. So, I started when I was 6.

We moved to another house after that. There were again a lot of problems between my mother and father. Subsequently, my father left. Then life became interesting because I no longer had to worry about what people thought of me. The more constant thought was how I was going to get money to buy food for the family (and I was only 9 years old, which was after the second rape by my uncle).

So, as I looked back, I saw that all of those events and the stories I told myself about those events were controlling my mind. These negative experiences from the past, that I had experienced already, were continuing to control my mind in the present.

Thus, as time passed, other negative experiences began to build upon and reinforce those stories – such as when a girl teased me, or when I was bullied. The only way that I could survive these stories of my life at that time was by reading books and escaping through other stories. That's how I kept this misthinking mind from bothering me. There were always things and events managing my mind. I was not in charge of my mind.

Eventually, these shortcomings, and society, became what was in charge of my mind. In later years (so-called manhood in age, not in evolvement), I thought that I was more intelligent than anyone else because nobody thought as much as I did. My mind had to create this rationalization because it was being dominated by society. This misthinking mind was always contemplating what I needed to do to be successful, to become whole, to become peaceful, and so on and so forth. What's worse, no matter how much I got of what this mind told me I needed, I never achieved the wholeness or peacefulness that was promised.

After getting into development and attaining the happiness I had been seeking for, I began to see the insanity in these old ways of misthinking. I could now recognize misthinking. As a result, I am able to manage my mind the vast majority of the time. The way that I manage my mind is that when certain insane thoughts come to me, or certain derogative things come to me, I know what to do with them. Usually, my level of interference from the mind that used to be in charge is just seconds. In real tough times, sometimes it can go on for a minute or two.

But hell, that's heaven!

All I could ever experience before was trouble, constant uneasiness, and not being able to sleep more than 4 or 5 hours because there was so much stuff running through my head. It used to be that when I went to bed, it would sometimes take me an hour and a half to go to sleep, if I could go to sleep at all! I remember a few years ago, I was telling my friend that I go to sleep in 3 minutes. When my wife happened to hear that, she screamed, "BS! He goes to sleep in 3 seconds!" So, that's kind of the way that life is today.

I'm truly blessed because I have come to know that everything I have developed and experienced has been by the miracle of GOD in my life. I have come to see without a shadow of a doubt that *GOD was taking care of me* before when I was an ignorant human being, is taking care of my life when I still do dumb things and will always take care of me because he's done it before. I have total trust about Him. I have faced death during my development through different circum-stances, and it wasn't any big deal.

Society is no longer in charge of my life. The misthinking mind has not been in charge of my life for quite a few years. The way I know this fact is true in my life is that life continues to get better.

But, who knows?

Maybe the next time you hear from me, you will hear me communicate that my mind was actually in charge and it was dominated by society for only a second. Regardless, the peacefulness that I experience today and the enjoyment I experience is amazing. I still make errors and mistakes. Now I have a GOD of my understanding, which is to stay that I stand safely in that understanding. Even when I do stupid things, I don't need to beat up on myself because GOD is in charge. The GOD that I have, of my understanding, has total forgiveness for me as well as everyone else. I benefit because I know this spiritual principle and I'm sure you will also when you practice that.

I wish you the best in your discovery, which means to search and study, in seeing how you have not been in charge of your mind, how society has ruled you, and finally how you can feel good about eliminating that society from your mind.

GOD bless you.

(How come when I want to go to sleep I start to worry about PMS (Power, Money, and Sex) and cannot stop these thoughts, even when I need the rest? How come I cannot stop from bothering myself?)

Chapter 9

The Power of Gratitude

When I pray, my prayers are those of gratitude. Why? Because everything I want or need has already been granted. Every precious gift was given at the foundations of the earth, and it is the Father's good pleasure to give you His kingdom.

GOD has put a table in front of me, a smorgasbord of gifts, opportunities, and things I might want or desire. From this table, I can choose anything I want. But depending on what I choose, or how I decide to get it, there will be a consequence.

I may choose a particular goal, and I can choose how I wish to reach that goal. I can choose to do so through ways that are proper, and honorable, and honest. . . or I can choose the opposite. I can choose to be improper, dishonorable, and dishonest. I still may get to my goal, but what that goal is going to give me at that point may not be what I was looking for.

Because whenever I want something badly, that's how I get it – **badly**.

At the beginning of my development, I practiced gratitude and made a daily habit of writing down things for which I was grateful. Current research suggests it take up to six weeks to develop a habit, and for that habit to become automatic. I don't know exactly how long I practiced writing down things for which I was grateful, but I know it was a phase I went through, and when I stopped, it wasn't because I stopped practicing gratitude, but because I had become grateful.

Another way in which I developed gratitude was by meditating. Through various practices, I was able to see the nature of my savage ignorance. I was self-centered in my thoughts and behaviors, I was narcissistic, and everything was about me.

I meditated on this, and looked at my life, and where I was in that moment, and asked myself if I really had the right to have experienced as much good as I had.

As a person who grew up without a mother (because my mother was around, but she wasn't there), without a father (I recall seeing my father maybe a half-dozen times), having only gone to grammar school, having been raped, having been bullied, having been made to feel less-than by many people at all stages of my life. . . a person with my upbringing and level of education normally could not have accomplished and experienced all I have.

In my daily living, whether I'm doing a lot or a little, whether I'm doing something, or nothing at all, one of the things I'm most grateful for is that I no longer bother me. When I'm writing this book, I'm writing this book. I'm here, **present** in the moment, and **conscious.**

I'm grateful in the knowledge that I am what I am, and what I am is enough. I no longer feel less-than, or insecure, because I have a GOD I rely on, and He has been taking care of me, is taking care of me, and will always take care of me.

When I was around 3 years in my development, I was listening to someone say the second most insane thing that I've ever heard. This person was communicating that *'nothing bad has ever happened in my life.'*

When I heard that, immediately my mind said 'you mean to tell me when I was raped twice, when my father left, when I went hungry, when all those things occurred, that wasn't bad?'

To which, he continued saying 'nothing bad has ever happened in my life because everything that has happened brought me to where I am today, and where I am is a wonderful place.'

As a result of hearing that, I began to see that in fact nothing bad has ever happened in my life – ***thank GOD for that.***

So, I'm grateful to know that nothing bad has ever happened in my life, because everything that has happened has brought me to where I am today. More important, those experiences brought me to **who I am** today, and who I am is great.

I thank GOD for that.

Good for Nothing

I don't know how many people can be reached, but I have hope that many people will find this book helpful.

I don't wish for anyone to suffer as much as I suffered as a result of my own stupidity and ignorance. I have come to see that until the age of 37, instead of having a mind that was working for me, I had a mind that was destroying me. Subsequently, I needed to put my mind to work, the same way one would put an employee to work. I would never hire an employee, and then do everything that employee told me to do. Would you? Yet, that's how I behaved with my mind.

What I love most about my life is when I wake up in the morning, I simply wake up. There are no little birds inside my head saying, ***You need to do this. You need to do that. You needed to do that yesterday! What are you going to do now?***

What I do today, from the moment I wake up in the morning, until I go to sleep at night, is breathe in and out. I do whatever I choose to do in front of me, or not. I have a relationship with GOD, and GOD does not punish me. Nor do I punish myself. When I do something wrong (which I do on a daily basis, as I have not achieved perfection), I make an effort to correct it, especially if it pertains to someone else. I can still be a little neglectful to me sometimes, but that's okay. I have a GOD of unconditional love, and I ceased playing GOD and beating up on myself many years ago.

The main reason I stopped playing GOD was because I saw that I was never qualified to do so. As a result of my giving up that role, I get to live a life in which I do whatever I want, whenever I want, as long as those actions are positive. There are certain things I still want to accomplish, such as this book, but those things are occurring as they occur. The speed at which they occur is proportional to my effort, but I don't set time limits, because I've found that when I do, I usually don't meet them. As I stated earlier, when I decide to do something, I never look to see how long it will take or how difficult it will be.

I just put one foot in front of the other, and when it's finished, it's finished.

I once heard a man say that the best one can be is to be good for nothing. When I first heard this, I thought he was bananas. But then he went on to explain himself.

The best thing one can be is to be good for nothing. Not for any reason. Not for any reward. He went on to explain that anything one does to an end is self-robbery. Even doing good because I want to go to Heaven is self-robbery. *I should simply be good for the sake of being good.*

I have often achieved the level of being good for nothing, and I am quite proud of it. Not all the time, of course, but more times than not.

If there is a *more* I still seek and desire, it is this; I would like to become one of GOD's greatest lovers of humankind, and the way I would like to become that is by possibly providing a window to the realization that I had so many years ago. I have suffered a great deal as a result of my own ignorance, and stupidity, and the lack of teaching that surrounded me. My hope is to help someone overcome their personal suffering more quickly than it took me.

Working With Pride

As mentioned before, after the divorce and the surrender of the furniture business, I went to work at Just Brakes. This was in 1987, I believe. I wasn't there that long, perhaps a couple of months. After that, I did management consulting for a company in Chicago.

I had seen an advertisement in a newspaper, so I applied. First, the company sent me for a week of training in Chicago, but when I arrived, they couldn't find any of my paperwork.

They told me to go through the course, anyhow. What the job consisted of was meeting with business owners, a review of their accounting and statements, and talking about the problems they were having with their business. The objective was to get them to sign up for our services, which, in 1987, cost $105 per hour, with a minimum of 100 hours.

I understood people well by that time, and the problem with a business is never the business. The problem with a business is always the same one; the owner.

So I went to my first job and met with the owner of the business. By the time the meeting was over, the company had signed up for 250 hours. I got a big congratulations from the main office, where they celebrated, and blew a horn. But when I got home and opened my mailbox, I found a letter from the very same company that had just congratulated me on my success.

The letter said they could not have me as a consultant because I didn't have the necessary requirements for the position, which was a college degree. It went on to say that I could apply to be a salesperson because that position did not require a degree. The salespeople were the ones who went to the business first to try to get them to agree to meet with one of the consultants.

So, I called my supervisor and said, "We're going to have to cancel this job."

He asked what the hell I was talking about, so I told him, "I'm not working for the company."

Again, he asked, "What are you talking about?"

"Well," I said, "when I got home, I found a letter saying I couldn't do the job I just did. It told me I could apply to be a salesperson, but not a consultant."

To which he replied, "Ah, screw that. Continue doing what you're doing."

I did, and I was relatively successful at it, but after a while, I began to notice that some of the jobs I had retained were being canceled on the first day that our people went to do the work. So after one meeting, I decided to stay and meet up with the person who was going to do the job. It was when I did this that I realized why the businesses were canceling. The people they had doing the work were dummies, and business owners are not dummies.

It was then that I quit.

When I came to this country, I thought the president and Ann Margaret would be waiting for me at the airport. They were not, and the following day I was working as an electrician's helper.

When I began to do that work, I could not speak English. I couldn't even understand English, so I started two steps below the first floor. Even though I had hated everyone I had worked for up to that point (with the exception of one uncle), one of the things that was inculcated in me, even though it was unconscious to me, was that whatever I did, I needed to do my best.

I didn't know at the time that this is called working with pride.

People sometimes think that pride is a bad word, but it's good to have pride. The only time that something similar to that becomes wrong is when I'm **prideful** or **prideless**. Prideful is arrogance. Prideless is carelessness. Both of those extremes are just as demeaning to myself, as well as those around me. **It's about balance.**

In my personal life, I never had any manageability within myself, but at work, I found that whenever I was there, I was fully there. In my personal life, I was never present because I was always thinking about either the future or the past. The structure of work, of being somewhere and having a specific task to do, gave me a sense of focus. Conversely, when I was alone in my off hours, the whole world was open wide for me, and my mind went nuts with it.

The two things that promoted my wellbeing at work was that I worked with pride, and I knew that two plus two equals four. I didn't try to make three or five out of it. Life really can be that simple.

After quitting the job as a management consultant, I bought a Mexican restaurant with my cousin, and we did that for three or four years before selling it because he wanted to get out. After that, I bought an Italian restaurant with another business partner and did that for about five years.

And then, at the end of '98, I started another furniture business.

But whether I was working for someone else, working for myself, or working *on* myself, *I have always worked with pride.*

(Instead of me asking another question, I'd like you to insert something of your own here. What insights into yourself and your mind have displayed for you as a result of reading this book? What would you like to change? Please pick two or three behaviors that you would like to change about yourself.)

Chapter 10

Waking Up

The best thing I did in my first year of development was *I didn't listen to me*. I studied. I sought mentorship. I accumulated vast amounts of information from a variety of sources, which I could then begin piecing together. Once I arrived at a certain point, I was able to put all of that knowledge to use.

Getting to that point was not the arrival, it was the beginning of the journey. It's like when we first wake up in the morning. Our eyes open and we're here. Perhaps we look at the alarm clock, or the ceiling, or the window for a moment. Then we raise ourselves from the bed and stand. Next, we have to use the restroom and put on the coffee, but we're still not awake, yet.

It's the same with development.

It's tiring to fight with life. And looking back, I did a lot of fighting. I was fighting for objects. I was fighting for status. I was fighting for feelings. There was a constant disturbance — a constant bother.

It took me too long to realize the most bothersome thing in my life used to be me. I used to be constantly fighting with myself, and I always lost.

I had to learn how to **surrender to win**.

Japan surrendered to the Allies and it was an unconditional surrender. How are they doing now? Currently, Japan is 3rd in global economic status, behind only China and the United States.

In our society (and the whole world, as well), there isn't a single piece of education that tells us how to utilize the brains GOD has given to us. What we hear instead is, ***you got to get this, you got to get that, you got to be this, you got to be that, and you'll never be happy until you get more, more, more!***

The accumulation of society's false ideas doesn't stop. Not, at least, until it's changed. The only difference between me starting my development at 37, versus 20, or 60, is the amount of junk I'm going to have to get rid of. The older one gets, the more junk one accumulates.

We often look for a solution to life, but no single solution fixes everything. What I use to fix a flat cannot be used to repair a blown engine. This goes back to specifics and generalities. A flat and a blown engine are both specifics that can be fixed. Simply saying there is something wrong with the car is a generality, and it will get me nowhere.

The reason we search for the key to life is because if we can find it, then we won't have to do anything else. So we live searching for that key in hopes of finally becoming happy and at peace.

There is a person whom I have never met, but I admire very much, and one of his sayings is, "What I came looking *for*, I came looking *with*."

Life is supposed to be free and happy. Today, my life is free and happy, but I needed to remove all of the things that were blocking me from that happiness. It was only when I got rid of those things that the true flourishing could begin.

Growing up, I cannot recall a single truly happy person in my life.

There was one who appeared to be the kind of person I wanted to be like. He was a relative of mine. He helped everyone and seemed to be a free person, but in his 50s he began to develop depression. He was not a happy camper. He and his wife were true worshippers of the Catholic religion, but neither had any freedom. So even the one whom I thought had it did not, as evidenced by the outcome later in life.

The closest we get to happiness quite often is we see a few serious people who say they have it together. And GOD, if happiness is that serious, let me find something else.

Freedom comes from my trust in GOD, which was another thing I had to learn.

If I don't trust in GOD, then I must be GOD. And if I am GOD, then I have proven that I am a lousy GOD. I have no power, and I've made myself miserable.

Take, for example, my rapes, and the subsequent things that happened that took away my trust. There is only one thing worse than trusting and being disappointed, and that is never to trust at all. Since I have become a relatively balanced person, I truly have been ripped off more than ever before. But because of my trust in GOD, everything that has been stolen from me, or that I was cheated out of, has been replaced, and more. And that's because I just trusted. I haven't lived in terms of lacking for over 30 years.

I even trusted when I felt I was dying. That's a lot of trust. And there's still more trust for me to develop in certain areas. I would like to tell you that I walk on water, but that only happens in the shower. Life is really good, so long as I choose to cooperate with it. And that's the key. I choose to cooperate with it.

Not fight.

Not struggle.

Surrender to win.

There's only one way to develop trust, and that's by trusting. There's an old statement that says, **if you wait to know before you go, you'll never go**.

You go, and then you know.

And then there is the question that comes to me whenever I'm reluctant about doing something. "Richard, if not now, when?"

I trust others, not because I have faith in them, but because I have faith in GOD. No matter what others do, I'm alright. Because I believe that GOD **has been** taking care of me, **is** taking care of me, and **will always** take care of me.

And the reason I believe this is because I've come to see that's how it was, is, and will always be.

Escaping

Until the age of 37, my mind had been destroying me. As a result of my own ignorance, and stupidity, and foolish behavior, I suffered tremendously.

I don't wish that on anyone, and that is why I'm writing this book.

The mind that was **working me** (rather than working **for** me) was not my own. It was the mind of society. It was a mind operating on insecurities, rather than the intelligence GOD had given me.

I didn't know that my mind was supposed to work for me, just like my legs and arms were supposed to work for me. I never went to any school (nor have I heard of any school) that teaches these principles. Nobody ever taught me that thinking was for constructing. No one ever showed me how my misthinking was the root of my suffering – and the suffering I caused to those around me.

And the reason no one ever taught me these things was because they didn't know, either.

I needed to find out (and thank GOD I did at the age of 37!) that my mind was supposed to be an employee of mine, and I was supposed to be the one in charge. Not my past experiences, or my insecurities, or my traumas.

I had to find out who was in charge of my mind.

And then I had to **take charge** of my mind.

This is what we need to teach our children. We need to teach them that their minds are theirs and that their minds are supposed to promote them. We need to show them how to replace negativity with positivity, and show them that they have the ability to choose between helpful thoughts, and harmful thoughts, between automatic reactions, and deliberate actions. And we need to teach them how to be **happy**.

In our society, we are taught to **get** and that **getting better things** is the path to **happiness**. When I was growing up, **more** was the answer. And if I were able to acquire all of the **mores** I was told about, then I would be happy.

But never once did anyone tell me what would be **enough**.

We are taught to be human **getters**, not human **beings**, and nobody can get all of the **mores** that exist.

If you get a Rolls Royce, what about a Lamborghini?

What about a Bugatti?

How about a cruise ship? Or an airplane?

We have to stop giving to our children without any effort of their own and start teaching them how to work.

I'm glad I started as a poor boy because I learned to work and to accomplish things, rather than wait on someone to do them for me. I have received the rewards of working with pride.

And yet, even in my own family, I have made the same errors society makes. I have given when it was not called for, and that has served to the detriment of some of my family members.

Rather than telling students (or adults, for that matter) what they need to acquire to be happy, we need to impress upon them the importance of actions and consequences, and the dangers of trying to escape from life, whether that is through alcohol, drugs, or even something as seemingly innocent as entertainment.

I have tried to escape life. I tried with drugs a few times, I tried with alcohol, and I tried with sex, but I could not escape *me*. I wanted to escape because I felt an emptiness inside of myself, and as long as that was occurring, I was never able to live life.

If we want to evolve, if we want to teach our kids how to be happy, rather than *get more*, we should begin by teaching them two things.

First, we need to show them how the mind works, how it's supposed to work for them, and how to communicate their feelings.

Second, we need to teach them about spiritual principles, primarily *what you sow you reap*.

There is no reward without effort and no true satisfaction without work. But this is not what we're teaching our children, and this is what I believe needs to change.

We have our minds at our disposal, and we can use them to better ourselves, to better our world, and to better our lives. All we need to do is use them as GOD intended, and all I needed to do was learn what wasn't taught — either in school or in society at large.

The development I have experienced has been the best adventure I have ever known. May you continue to have the enthusiasm to pursue your own development, and to experience the greatest adventure you could ever know.

(Who's in charge of my mind? How is it that at times I have no control over what my mind does? Its thoughts take me all over the place. In the past, it would take me wherever it wanted to go for as long as it wanted to. Why isn't my mind, mine?)

Chapter 11

Who's in charge of my mind?

One of the ways that I could know when my mind was in charge of me was by looking to see what was going on inside of my head. For instance, if I went to bed and I couldn't sleep because one or more things were running through my head, then my head was in charge of me because I wanted to go to sleep.

Whenever I'm driving on the highway and I'm concerned about the traffic or other drivers or how long is it going to take for me to get there and on and on and all of that music that goes on inside of the head, well for sure I'm not using my mind – it's using me. Because I know today that the traffic is going to do what the traffic is going to do, and it makes no sense to be stressed out about anything.

There's an old saying: 'worrying is like a rocking chair, it will give me something to do, but it will get me nowhere.' It's the same thing about me getting concerned about traffic, or the weather, or anything at all.

It's the same as when I go to the store and the line is not going fast enough to satisfy me. Even though I have no place to go, these people are still not doing it right. I know in these moments that my head is not working for me either, that I'm working for it.

Because one of the things that I also know the same as traffic is that I have no power to control other people. I have no power to control people or traffic, *yet I do have the control over how I react to whatever occurs.*

For that, I have total power - when I am utilizing my mind.

When it's utilizing me, that's another story.

Whenever I am unhappy it's because my mind, my old mind, has determined that something is not right for me: I don't have the looks; or I don't have the money; or I don't have this or that.

I know for sure that negativity does not produce happiness. I cannot get to good emotions through bad emotions.

What I have come to know regarding happiness is that the best way to be happy is to be grateful. Grateful not only for what I have, but also for what I continue to receive that is very good as far as I'm concerned.

The only thing that has changed in my life for the last 33 years is that each year has become better than the previous one. And it has been that way for 33 years plus. In all these years, I've only gotten divorced, gone from rich to poor to well off again, remarried. And as you can see from the stories in this book, I've been experiencing a dull life, right?

The key is that I've got to continuously remind myself in the beginning that anything that is negative - anything that is producing stress - needs to change. When I am aware that it needs to change, I am able to change it. I still don't control what comes into my mind, but I manage my mind most of the time. As soon as I hear negative thoughts from the old repertoire, I correct them in seconds with positive thoughts

Gratefulness is the way to happiness.

Before I used to have a lot of problems because I was trying to manage the whole world. I don't know how I came to the conclusion that I was supposed to be GOD, but I can tell you that I was a very lousy GOD to myself and the world. For over 33 years now, I have lived knowing that the GOD there is, is far superior and better than anything that I have tried to be. ***And I trust that GOD of my understanding.***

I need to continue to align myself with positive people and positive things. If I don't have positive people in my life, then I could look to positive authors: Dr. Scott Peck, Vincent Peele, Dr. Joseph Murphy and Father John Doe, as examples. I have associated myself with many different sources to develop the good life that I have today. For that purpose, the books needed to be positive.

What I needed to do the most, to be able to do what I'm doing today, was begin to face up to any inadequacies that I saw happening to me or within me. The more that I faced up to those things and the more I removed them, the better my life has gotten. And it continues to be wonderful today.

Sometimes I don't want to say anything because it just seems like I'm bragging. But, well, I've never had it so good.

I've just got to thank GOD. And I do thank GOD for all good things which happen in my life. On some occasions in my past, the worst thing that I have said was 'GOD, I don't know how I got into this, but please get me out of it!' And it has not been GOD's fault.

Before I arrived at the level of development that I have today, it seemed like I blamed everything else and everyone else, including GOD. I never accepted the blame, even though I was the one doing those things. It's amazing how much fault I place on GOD, without Him doing anything.

But today, I am grateful that I have a GOD that I can rely on and trust. I have gone through so many things in the last 33 years. Most of the time, I am unharmed by any of those things.

The key is to realize that if I'm not happy my mind is not working for me. If I'm worried, stressed, or I can't go to sleep, then I'm working for my mind.

I have come to see without a shadow of a doubt that my mind used to be formed by the inadequacies of society - my shame, my fears, past experiences that were controlling my present life - before I developed.

To obtain freedom from that mind, I just need to continuously put one foot in front of the other. My desire is for no one to have to suffer out of their own delusions or illusions as much as I did for the first 37 years of my life.

Life is good... Once I learned to live it.

Thank GOD that today I live life. I am no longer surviving. For the first 37 years, I was surviving, and I wasn't dying. The last 33 plus years I have been living and continue to live on a daily basis. Life is wonderful within me and outside of me.

When I have a problem with my swimming pool, my swimming pool has a problem, not me. I just have to correct the problem with my swimming pool, not with me. And thank GOD that I usually have the means to take care of it.

The main thing that I want to emphasize is that my mind is supposed to operate for me, just like my legs, my arms, and my eyes. I determine what they do, and it is supposed to be the same way with my mind.

For instance, when I wake up in the morning, I do whatever I need to do. I put one foot in front of the other. I'm not concerned about anything. If there is anything that I'm concerned with when I get up in the morning, it might be the temperature in the room, if I need to adjust it. But outside of that, there are no concerns. *How is it with you?*

It used to be when I woke up in the morning, between the bed and the bathroom,

I went around the world with 50 things going through my head: what I needed to do; what I should've done; the pleasures I wanted to receive; what I wanted to get; who wasn't doing it for me; and who I wasn't doing it for either. It was just like the 24 hours of Le Mans every day in my head.

Today, all I've got to do is just wake up and put one foot in front of the other. If I have an appointment, I take care of it - sometimes I remember it, sometimes I forget, but that's ok.

One of the greatest things about being in charge of my mind today is, and I'm going to be as simple as I can be, I'm not a royal pain in the ass to me. It used to be that it was horrible the way that I treated myself in my head. Today, that's not the way it is.

By the way, with the GOD of my understanding, I always know when I am hearing a great communication because it is something too intelligent to be me. Also, when I am communicating with Him, whatever I hear back inside of me is positive.

If it isn't positive, it isn't GOD. It is the old mind from the old society. And I just don't listen to my old mind.

The key is I don't take myself too damn seriously, and I don't take them too damn seriously either.

And when everything else fails, love them whether they can understand it or not... And that's not one of the things that I normally say. I call that rule 64. If you want to know about rule 64, you have to talk to me personally.

So rule 62: I don't take myself too damn seriously.

Rule 63: I don't take them too damn seriously.

And rule 64 is for private consumption.

So anyhow – I'm enjoying life today and all that I can say is: if you're not enjoying life, you have not learned to see how it is that you are making it not enjoyable.

In conclusion, even though a spiritual advisor or teacher is important, actually the most important part is being a student. Just like Einstein needed to first be a student, it was the quality of his effort that allowed him to surpass his teachers.

The mind I possessed for many years was the result of all the fears I experienced as a child and all the shame I felt within me. Sometimes it was just a feeling without any face, but nevertheless, ***this mind and these feelings were ruining my life.***

When all of those thoughts and fears became attached to society, society multiplied them by the thousands, and I had no way to fix any of it. I couldn't fix my own life because there was no one around me who knew how to fix theirs. They all seemed to be going through similar circumstances.

Unfortunately, far too many people still live that way. No matter where I go, I don't see shining, smiling faces. I'm lucky if I see one in fifty.

There has never been a time such as this, in which so many people are going in so many different directions. It used to be that society fought a couple of derogative ideas at a time, and now it seems that we have been overrun with this type of thinking.

That's how it used to be inside my head; too many thoughts going in too many directions.

Our minds are our most powerful tool, and one which can be utilized to achieve happiness. Yet, when I meet with young people, or old people, or poor people, or even multimillionaires, the one thing they have in common is that they are not happy. I have a friend over 80 years old who's still chasing the dollar, worried and stressed. . . and he's a multimillionaire! I always ask him, "What are you going to worry about when you're old?"

When I embarked on this journey, I fell in love with my development. The more I got into my development, the more I loved the peace, serenity, and happiness that resulted from my efforts. And the more I rejoiced in what I was receiving, the more I did - and continue to do - what is necessary to achieve more of those good feelings. *Today, it's still a pleasure, not a job*. In fact, it was never a job for me, which is not the common sentiment I hear from others. *For me, it is a wonderful adventure.*

But I couldn't put in the efforts just to be okay. If I had stopped when I felt okay, it wouldn't have been enough, and I would have found myself back where I started.

My life is so good today. I'm not fully in charge of my mind, but I am able to manage it most of the time. When I get a negative or derogative thought, two things happen almost immediately.

Number one, I laugh at the thought.

Number two, I change it.

I don't dwell on it. I don't ask where the thought came from. And I don't tell myself *you've been doing this over 30 years, you're supposed to be better than that*, because I've stopped playing GOD with myself. I simply change my thoughts and move on.

The thoughts that remain, and that I choose to maintain, are positive ones. And amazingly, when I have positive thoughts, I am happy. Before, happiness always came with a stipulation. I'll be happy *when*. . .

And *when* never came, and even if it did, I would always find another *when*.

Today, my life on a daily basis is tranquil, and I'm not affected by my thoughts. . . or the thoughts of *society*.

We need to begin teaching that the mind is a tool, and we need to start with our children. We need to help them understand that thinking is for constructing, not destroying ourselves or others. The more we utilize our minds for this purpose, the better our lives – and our world – will be.

P.S.

By the way, please remember the main object of this book was not to tell my story. It's to possibly show a way in which you can find the life that you have always searched for and wanted, just like I did. If you relate to what you're reading, you may find a way to get there yourself. I wish you very well in your journey.

Last, I don't know how you will assess this book. Do remember that it was written by a graduate of primary school, and even though I had examples of teachers, most of the time I was teaching myself.

So don't judge me too harshly.

If you think you are lacking the courage to evolve, just remember that if I can do it, anybody can do it.